Master Your Vibration

Edmund Harold is a clairvoyant channel, in addition to which he is an author and lecturer of some note, having spent the past fifteen years teaching esoteric subjects in several countries. The art of metaphysical healing is very dear to his heart having served in this caring field for some thirty years, twelve of which were spent at the helm of the Sussex Spiritual Healers Association in the United Kingdom.

In 1970 Edmund founded the Spiritual Venturers Association in Brighton, Sussex, an organisation which eventually spread to New Zealand and Australia, but in 1989 he also established the Bridge To Christ Consciousness in order to facilitate the creation of a centre for the study of metaphysical subjects, wherein those who seriously aspire to serve their fellow men and women may undergo a disciplined training in the mystical arts of seership and healing.

Master
Your
Vibration

Edmund Harold

Grail

Publications

First Published By Spiritual Venturers Education Trust, 1984.

Copyright Edmund Harold 1984: 1995:

This edition published in 1995 by Grail Publications,
P. O. Box 2316. Port Macquarie. NSW 2444.

Ilustrations by Leona Lal Singh.

Illustrations copyright Edmund Harold 1984.

Cover Design by Edmund Harold

National Library of Australia
Cataloguing-in-Publication data:

Harold Edmund.
Master Your Vibration.

ISBN 0 646 22385 2

Contents

Contents (cont.)

Preface

It is said that fact is often stranger than fiction and this is certainly true of what I have to share at this point in my narrative.   During the course of a lecture tour of New Zealand in 1981 I was persuaded to add several towns to my itinerary - places where I was assured there were many New Age thinkers, anxious to hear what I had to say on the subject of the impending earth changes.

The first of these talks attracted an audience of less than a dozen, almost half of whom formed part of my entourage. Naturally a little indignant at the poor response, this petulant Leo roared his disapproval and considered abandoning the event.

Common sense, coupled with a sense of duty, finally prevailed and I threw myself into my narrative with great gusto, ignoring the rows of empty seats.   As the subject was rather unpalatable (and possibly the reason for the empty seats), it was being accompanied that day by a talk on the role of the Ascended Masters in the future upheavals.

During this segment, as I held up a rough sketch of the Master R a gifted clairvoyant seated in the hall observed the said Master Soul manifest behind me, later describing in great detail the radiant aura of this Illumined One. I was also told that joining the Master upon the platform was the spirit form of my late mother, who acted as His intermediary.

I was - if he was to be believed - asked to consider undertaking the task of writing a book which detailed the role played by certain Ascended Masters in our lives, via the agency of the various numerical energies which so influence our everyday thoughts and emotional responses. In selecting my mother as intermediary it was obviously hoped that this would serve to convince me of the validity of the communication. In this it failed utterly, for I could not bring myself to accept my mother as the confidant of highly evolved beings.

However in the ensuing weeks my colleague was provided with more detailed information, the nature of which left me in no doubt as to its source. I then countered with a request for 'inspiration from on high' with regard to the exact nature of the role played by the Elder Brothers in our lives, for this was unknown to me. I also requested illustrations of The Illumined Ones in order that those who read the book might have a point of focus.

So began an eighteen month search for a suitable illustrator, for it would be so very easy to mislead in a subject of this nature. When two highly respected psychic artists finally admitted defeat after some fifteen months of effort, I advised the Higher Realms that I was no longer prepared to continue, in response to which I was advised "Write the book from the back!" As I did not fully comprehend this instruction, I chose to ignore it and set the project aside.

I then set out upon another lecture tour of New Zealand and once there, my spirit inspirers recommenced their communications. As I sat pondering the vagaries of life in downtown Wellington (where my lectures had again failed to attract large numbers of people) I was informed "we are ready to commence the latter part of the book". I sped back to my hotel and began to set down the mass of information which was now flowing quite freely. There was however, no information with regard to the the illustrations I required.

Upon arrival in Christchurch a friend who met my flight enquired about the book I was to write. I shared the tale and was advised that a friend of hers had suddenly commenced painting pictures of The Masters. I was totally unimpressed and changed the subject, for there are varying levels of psychic art, few of which I would care to embrace. The following week yet another friend told me of the wonderful work being undertaken by this artist, asking me to give her serious consideration. I refused, but in the ensuing days found myself highly pressured by both ladies to go and view the paintings.

On the understanding that the person concerned was to be given no advance warning of my visit or of its purpose I finally agreed. This was to ensure that I could beat a hasty retreat once I had viewed what I felt would prove to be illusionary flights of fancy.

Imagine my surprise when I cast my eyes upon the portrait of The Lord Maitreya, together with two others which were then the sum total of her work. I am uncertain which of us had the greater shock, for the artist - a shy, retiring woman had received instruction that she was to work with a man called Edmund Harold whom she would shortly encounter.

It was not until we later sat and compared notes that we discovered that we both were advised of our joint task on precisely the same day , although neither had been advised of the others participation in this task. It should also be noted that the artist has not received any professional training whatsoever during this present lifetime, although the works are completed in oils. She was also quite insistent that her name be omitted from the credits.

The ensuing months brought a great flurry of artistic activity for us both and when the artist exceeded the required number of illustrations I was forced to ask my 'mentors' for information on their purpose. The answer to that question was somewhat terse. "There is a further book to be written, one that will expand upon the message in the first. . . "

Footnote to Second Edition.

Following the original publication of this book I received many letters and comments upon it, ranging from the highly complementary to those which considered the illustrations to be astral in nature. These I accepted as fair comment as it is known that there are astral forms in existance, fashioned from the emotional thought patterns of those who, having heard of the Ascended Masters, longed to communicate with, and even meet them. In the light of these comments I would like to share the following story with you.

Some years after the release of this book I sat one day with my artistic friend, meditating in the 'Masters ' Room' within which the portraits of the Masters hung. This was a special room set aside for this purpose and the energies within it were quite powerful. As the meditation session drew to a close, a member of the White Brotherhood suddenly appeared in our midst. I enquired the reason for his presence and in reply he then pointed to the paintings upon the walls. "These" he said "are not portraits of the Ascended Masters."

My heart sank into my boots. For if this were true then I had been guilty of misleading many people and the eventual repayment was too great to contemplate. "What then are they ?" I whispered. Turning to me he said "They are representations of the energies of The Masters, intended only as a point of focus upon which those who desire to expand their level of awareness might meditate. In this manner it is hoped that all who do so might then endeavour to activate their spiritual potentials and eventually desire to take a quantum leap toward a higher level of consciousness. "

This statement called to mind a communcation I had received some years earlier from the Master R. when I became frustrated by my inability to obtain suitable illustrations for this book. "We no longer possess physical forms" He told me gently. "I do realise that" I replied " but those who read the book will require some form of identification." In reply the Master continued, "We no longer have etheric forms. Indeed, we no longer possess any physical energy which you might recognise as form." Undaunted I replied, "Without some type of image to focus upon, I doubt that the book would find an audience, so perhaps I should abandon the task." At this the communication ceased. . .

Acknowledgements

No work of this nature can truly be said to be the work of just one individual and I would therefore like to thank all of those who participated in its creation in one form or another, particularly those who gave me the necessary encouragement when my enthusiasm was flagging - which was fairly often.

In particular I extend my grateful thanks to the late Stephen Warne who through his written works and then later as a friend, helped me to re-discover the science of numerology. He was a man with a rare gift who could make this subject live as no other could.

To Alfred A. my deepest gratitude for it was his 'vision' which sparked off the whole concept - and for the further inspiration he later provided. Equally, I am deeply indebted to Leona without whom this book would not have seen the light of day - and those Enlightened Ones who so inspired her contribution . Without Bill L. and his insistence that the whole concept should be widened, I doubt that I would have proceeded, For his patience and caring attention I thank him.

On the production front I wish to thank David C. for his painstaking photography and Patricia Mary Walker for her patience in editing the manuscript, also Linda King for taking the time to peruse and correct the finished work. Above all, for the opportunity to serve I give grateful thanks to those all-wise Elder Brothers whose work this truly is.

Numerical Vibrations

Numerology is an exact science which serves to identify the various forms of energy which influence our emotional responses and actions in daily life. However, all energies are possessed of a positive and negative aspect and when we are faced with a difficult situation there is a tendency to take the line of least resistance reflecting thereby, the negative influence of the of the numeric vibration we are seeking to master.

Within this form of numerology (based upon the Pythagorean method) the numbers 1 to 5 - relating to independence, emotion, self-expression, will-power and thought control reflect attributes of the human nature, whilst those from 6 to 9 represent challenges for the Higher or Spiritual Nature, largely through selfless love for others, mysticism, initiation and service to mankind.

On a still higher level, the vibrations of 11 and 22 serve to awaken within the self an awareness of the necessity for a practical approach toward life and all humanitarian undertakings. As the lessons associated with the numbers 11 and 22 are infinitely more challenging, the individual will require great strength of character if they are to achieve success.

Those viewing this science for the first time may well feel daunted at the prospect of unwanted restraint on their freedom of thought and action and some among you may well resent the implication that growth may only be attained by assisting others to resolve their problems.

Reactions like these are understandable, for the majority among us tend to rebel when faced with such *faits accomplis*.. Fortunately the resentment rarely lasts and we tend to resume our normal, helpful characteristics, progressing toward our unknown goal. However, should resentment become deep seated, it can lead to a lowering of the physical vitality and eventually to ill health.

The science of numerology, together with its sister science of astrology, clearly indicates the Soul's journey through time and matter, whereby it may absorb the many lessons which the various energy vibrations, both numeric and planetary have to teach. Each individual soul will be presented with many opportunities to master these lessons during the course of the numerous physical embodiments that all must expect to experience on this Plane of Matter.

In common with astrology, numerology also has its hidden or *esoteric* aspect. Those souls who have incarnated in order to experience the reverse rotation of the Great Wheel of Life in a determined bid to overcome the pull of illusion, will also be expected to respond to the higher (or esoteric) vibration of the various numeric energies which govern their lives. The level of challenge will naturally be great, but so too will be the eventual reward. Study closely therefore the higher vibration of each number if you aspire to follow the *esoteric* pathway through life.

Reincarnation and the Law Of Karma.

The subject of reincarnation is one which sorely troubles many in the western hemisphere, for few care to embrace a concept which indicates a need to return to this Vale of Tears following the death of the current physical form. Within these pages you will note many references to this divisive subject, for the science of numerology provides a clear indication of previous embodiments in the world of matter.

If you are prepared to consider the possible influence of numeric energies upon your everyday thoughts and actions, there must already exist a sizeable chink in your armour of disbelief in relation to this most contentious of subjects.

Those who possess an open mind should stop for a while and take stock of themselves and their respective life patterns; note their current levels of sensitivity or whatever creative capacity they may possess and endeavour to divine their origin. They should also take a hard look at their present lifestyle, which differs so greatly from that experienced by many in the more populous regions of the world.

Most among us acknowledge a belief in God in some form or other and, despite attempts made by certain narrow christian sects to teach us to fear the Lord, most consider the Supreme Source of All Life to be the creative source of Love. If, as we are led to believe, we are all Children of the God of Love why then is there such great disparity evident within the living conditions of the various races of humanity? Surely not, because some worship a different form of God, for the rational thinkers know this to be one and the same force, worshipped under another name.

Why do many millions of people suffer deprivation, undergoing horrendous hardships, largely due to the worldly aims of power seekers, or are condemned to a brief and miserable existence because the abundance which does exist upon the Earth today is not equally shared? If there is only one life experience for each to undergo, there is something radically wrong on Earth and the God we profess to believe in cannot love all equally - unless of course, there has been an earlier existence within which the soul has merited the current experience of suffering. After all, the bible does refer to the concept of 'an eye for an eye. . . ' does it not?

The teaching of reincarnation has long been accepted and understood by the peoples of the East. Yet sadly, it has led to a deal of apathy among the majority who make little or no attempt to improve their quality of life, and set such action aside for yet another life experience.

Such negativity is possibly the reason why in AD 600 the bishops at the Council of Nicea, condemned the teachings of Origen and proceeded to strip the Christian faith of all references to reincarnation, which until that time had represented a major portion of the mystical teachings of The Christ. However some references eluded them for, in Matthew 11. v. 13 and v. 14 there is a clear reference to reincarnation.

To locate the answer to this most vexatious problem we must return to the biblical statement of an 'eye for an eye', which in the Eastern hemisphere is referred to as the Law Of Karma or, if you prefer, the Law of Cause and Effect. The Lord Buddha stated that the Law of Karma cannot be comprimised in any way and that karma follows man as surely as the cart follows the oxen. It represents that which we must all meet in the fullness of time.

As the result of this statement of the Lord Buddha, many who reach an awareness of an earlier life experience come also to fear the Law of Karma, even as the majority of Christians fear retribution on the Day of Judgment. Needless to say, each and every one among us has encountered the latter experience in some measure following the death of the physical self at an earlier point in our evolution and the karmic repayment exacted of us during the current lifetime reflects the decision of the Higher Self to repay part of its debt.

Karma, therefore, is not something to fear. Rather it is a golden opportunity for all evolving souls to rejoice in, being fully determined that, during the current life experience, they will attain a measure of self control through the conscious acceptance of the burdens they have elected to bear.

We do, of course, create karma on a daily basis; that which we think or do, and which in turn causes harm to another, begins to form a debit balance in our Akashic record (or Book of Life). This can (in a measure) be balanced once we reach an awareness of the power of thought and begin to review our thought patterns and actions at days end.

This is a relatively simple act whereby we review (in a detached manner) the events of the day, from its end back to its commencement. Where this review reveals a destructive (but unspoken) response to the thoughtless actions of another, we should endeavour to direct toward the injured party a counter thought pattern of 'Light' and this should be charged with' Unconditional Love' .

Should the projection of unconditional love prove to be difficult initially, try projecting a ray of rose pink light (the colour of unconditional love). Where we fail to follow such a course of action, our earlier destructive activity will be duly recorded upon our Akashic Record and stored as karma, to be repaid at some future point in time.

The outworking of the Law of Karma often appears to be grossly unfair to those who have no knowledge of earlier life experiences. Quite often these people are hardworking, supportive individuals who do no harm to others, yet throughout their lifetime they experience great suffering and all manner of hardship. Such experiences reflect karma accumulated over a number of earlier lifetimes and, where possible, this should be cheerfully borne. But where the response to such situations is anger or a deep resentment directed towards the Creator, this will merely serve to exacerbate their current suffering and create the potential for further repayment in a future life.

Finally, the Ancient Wisdom tells us that every act of each and every individual is recorded upon the Akashic Record and that from this self - created record flow the destinys of humanity and the nations which we establish. Therefore our present qualities and talents are born of that which we have ourselves set in motion in the long-gone past. Our thoughts and actions today will determine our future - the Law of Cause and Effect is immutable. As we sow, so shall we reap. . . Perfect justice for all!

The Purpose of Life

The first and most important lesson for all who seek their Reality lies in reaching an understanding of the fact that we are first and foremost spirit entities incarnate for a period of time in a physical form and the express purpose of incarnation being to experience all that which the world of matter has to offer. In turn, each individual soul has to attempt to raise the vibration of the physical form it currently inhabits.

All life springs from the Creative Source (The Father\ Mother God) and to that Source all must ultimately return, having experienced all illusionary situations en route. The science of numerology provides an indication of how the individual entity evolves through each level of vibration - to which a numerical identification has been applied. The following chart may aid those who ponder this subject.

Vibration	Energy and Potential Represented
1 Sun	This is the primary vibration, one found within all matter, serving to reflect the masculine aspect of the Father/Mother God
2 Moon	As the Moon reflects the light of the Sun this vibration reflects the feminine aspect of the Creator and requires the positive impulse of the 1 energy in order to bring about expansion.

Vibration	Energy and Potential Represented
3 Jupiter	Is born out of the union of 1 and 2 and reflects the impulse of the Third part of the Trinity (The Son)
4 Uranus	Reflects the unknown into which the spirit entity is projected in order that it may learn to express itself.
5 Mercury	Provides the opportunity to explore the dimension of the mind.
6 Venus	Offers the opportunity to reflect the Higher Self through a loving disposition.
7 Neptune	Provides the stimulus to communicate with the non-physical dimensions.
8 Saturn	Presents the restrictive situations and opposition so very necessary for all would-be initiates.
9 Mars	Stimulates the realisation that selfless service to humanity is vital in order to evolve.
11 Pluto	Tests the individuals' ability to put idealism into action in a practical manner.
22 Vesta	Offers the opportunity to relate in a conscious way to the Creator via humanitarian undertakings.

Taking this one step further, each numerical force is possessed of a positive aspect representing the ultimate goal (or Esoteric challenge) to be achieved by all who are subject to each vibration. The following guidelines may assist.

Number	Quality	Attainment
1	Independence	Leadership
2	Harmony	Adaptability
3	Self Expression	Growth
4	Practicality	Self Discipline
5	Communication	Self Control
6	Loving	Responsibility
7	Sensitivity	Seership
8	Business Acumen	Success
9	Benevolence	Service
11	Idealism	Practicality
22	Humanitarianism	Self-Mastery

Numbers are a means of identifying particular forms of energy to which we are all subject from time to time during the course of our lives. In addition to their positive aspect all energies also have a negative pole. Human nature being what it is, we tend to take the line of least resistance when faced with a measure of difficulty or the need to make a decision, responding quite readily to the negative aspect of any numeric vibration. However such activity merely serves to impede our progress and ensures that the lesson will have to be repeated at some future point in time.

It is also important to realise that we are all subject to the influence of various numeric vibrations during the course of our lifetime, some of which may well serve to inhibit the expression of our finer qualities.   To reach an undertanding of just what these impediments are and how you may in turn come to master them, it is suggested that a chart be compiled, based upon the date of birth and given names at birth.   In the following pages the student will be shown how to construct such a chart.

The Illumined Ones

The ultimate goal for all of mankind is to become the master of self and of matter, such acts leading eventually to the conscious acceptance of a portion of responsibility for the planet upon which we currently gather our experience. As the very early races of mankind showed a marked reluctance to accept such responsibilites, there appeared upon the earth Elder Brothers - Illumined Ones, drawn from other galaxies, to guide the slowly evolving races toward self-realisation.

Their unselfish devotion to the requirements of humanity has borne fruit in the form of a group of souls who, of themselves, have sought to master the illusions which abound in this world of matter, accepting therein the many hardships and disciplines attendant within the search for total self-mastery. The Bible refers to these beings as 'The Very Elect'. Today we know them as The Ascended Masters, although they themselves, now beyond the pull of matter and ego, prefer to be known as our Elder Brothers and Sisters.

As individuals we laboriously endeavour to attain higher levels of spiritual awareness and it soon becomes evident that greater teachers are necessary if we are to continue to evolve so the search for such teachers commences. This, more often than not, is doomed to failure for mankind must first earn the right to such knowledge. A great many today clutch at straws in the wind, seeking not to master self but merely to follow blindly the dictates of another. Such acts are escapism and are unacceptable on higher levels of consciousness.

At some point within that which we term time, all must take up the path of self-mastery and seek to become Initiates of the Temples of Truth. Within the long-lost civilisations of this planet, and throughout what were often long and difficult lifetimes, many who read these words commenced rigorous training and embraced stern disciplines as they entered into temple life as neophytes, learning therein to balance the energies within the self.

Those mystery schools no longer exist as such on the physical plane and our search for self mastery is therefore more arduous, as we must endeavour to attain complete self-control whilst surrounded by all manner of negativity and illusion. Each lifetime is a fresh attempt upon the summit of total consciousness, within which we must again endeavour to seek the Inner Reality and rid ourselves of illusionary ties.

Within these pages is shared information which illust-rates the futility of a long and fruitless search for a Master, for is it not written 'when the pupil is ready the Master will appear?' The individuals who seek to master self through the control of the energies which flow through their lives, will in turn attract the attention of those Illumined Ones whose vibration closely corresponds to the positive aspect of the energies with which they currently do battle. The knowledge shared herein comes with the hope that it will aid the overall growth of all who read it.

Currently, information regarding the Ascended Masters is beginning to filter through to the people of the West in order that they might be provided with a personal goal upon which they may fix their attention. It is emphasised however that the Illumined Ones **do not** wish to be worshipped or idolised, for they consider themselves to be but our Elder Brothers and Sisters who have travelled this arduous path a little longer than most and in so doing have attracted greater responsibilities. We in turn must seek to share the enlightenment we receive through the agency of such Beings as we battle our way toward Reality. Such is the Law of Sequence and Consequence.

This book is the first of two which I have undertaken to complete on the behalf of the Illumined Ones. Within the first of these I endeavour to illustrate how each in turn might master self through the realisation that the numeric vibrations which influence our lives serve to illustrate the path towards greater reality. Within the second of the series I will attempt to illustrate the pitfalls which await along the Path of Discipleship - which sees the need for all to embrace many different forms of initiation.

Footnote to Second edition:

This further volume still remains to be completed, largely due to a forewarning that should I not be completely accurate in what I set down, there would be serious consequences. This was sufficient for me to set the task aside, but now, some ten years on, I feel more confident in my ability to undertake this work and it will be commenced in the not too distant future.

Female Adepts

On learning of the existence of Masters or Illumined Beings, many query why there appear to be no women among their ranks - a natural comment in this day of female emancipation. There are of course female Adepts (a better description than Master, with its masculine overtone I feel,) but their role differs from that of the male Adepts. In esoteric teaching the female is considered to represent the feminine principle of the Supreme Source of All Life and it is the sensitive qualities of intuition and inner vision - so sadly ignored in today's world - that the female Adepts will endeavour to re-awaken within all of mankind.

Among their number is one outstanding Adept known within the Christian belief as Mary, Mother of the Master Jesus, who has an important role to play in the development of New Age thinking. Mary will also assist in the total emancipation of women, leading them to assume their rightful role during the Age of Aquarius, wherein they will become the true leaders of the race, heading the new civilisations which will need to be established following the downfall of our current corrupt civilisations.

The Illumined Being whom we know today as Mary undertook many initiations within the temples of Atlantis, but it was the later initiations undertaken in Egypt within the Temple of Isis (where She eventually became High Priestess) which led to her current Mastership status.

There are others who are within sight of the final stages of self - mastery, among them the soul known as St. Teresa of

Avila who brought about many reforms within the Catholic Church, and who is set to emerge to the fore within the New Age. She links with mankind on the Ray of Intellect and brings awareness of the necessity to embrace a new religion, one based upon complete acceptance of our Oneness with the Supreme Source of All Life, coupled with a new form of theology. To this end She currently endeavours to bring about a widening of outlook within those presently heading spiritual orders.

The being we know as St. Catherine of Sienna also made appearances as the historical figure Joan of Arc and later returned as Helena Blavatsky, the founder of the Theosophical movement. Within the Age of Aquarius this soul has a fresh and vital role to play in stimulating spiritual outgrowth within mankind.

The Radiant One, who Christianty refers to as St. Clare, has an equally important role to play in mankind's search for greater spiritual awareness and during the New Age will reincarnate in order that she may assist in the preparation of the way for the Aquarian Christ. Interestingly enough, His earthly channel will be the Ascended Master Kuthumi, who is the male counterpart of St.Clare.

The Lord Maha Chohan

The Lord Maha Chohan, known as the Lord of Civilisation, is linked with the number 0, which of itself corresponds to conception. This was the numerical vibration which governed the long-lost continent of Lemuria and its subsequent civilisation.

The number 0 relates to each of the races which will need to undergo total extinction before the end of the current Age of Pisces. It equally represents the death of the physical form, whilst our Planet Earth also resonates to the vibration of this number.

All those who are born on the 10th: 20th: and 30th draw towards them the strengthening energies of the Lord Maha Chohan, which in turn will encourage the intensification of all positive qualities within their respective natures.

His influence will create the potential for expansion of those personal lessons which are illustrated within the Governing Factor lesson of each respective individual ie: those who are born on the 10th must seek to intensify the lessons which the number 1 seeks to teach ie: independence and leadership, by demonstrating total independence of thought and action and the development of positive or dynamic leadership qualities.

Those born on the 20th will need to expand upon the lesson which the number 2 teaches, ie: learning to adapt to their environment and controlling their emotional responses. These individuals must demonstrate not only their capacity to move with the tide of public opinion, but also their complete adaptability in any given situation - utilising their skilful diplomatic abilities where necessary. Finally, those who are born on the 30th must further develop the lesson attached to the 3 vibration - which in itself encourages expansion and growth. This they can achieve by stretching themselves and expanding their artistic or creative abilities demonstrating to the world at large just how outstanding their particular talents are.

Currently the Lord Maha Chohan's sphere of influence lies within the intensification of awareness of the powers of the Mineral Kingdom, and all who draw His attention will find that the study and usage of minerals to benefit the evolution of the human race, will assume a great importance in their lives.

Equally, as His energies relate to that which is still to unfold upon the Earth, His disciples will be encouraged to raise the level of their intellect and to expand their conscious awareness of the link between mind and spirit.

The Lord Maha Chohan

The Master Hilarion

Linking with the higher vibration of the number 1, the Ascended Master Hilarion brings a new beginning and a fresh sense of purpose to those who come under His influence. The thrust of His energies will stimulate positive action and the expression of individuality, and all who are born on the 1st: 10th: 19th: and 28th will greatly benefit from His influence, as will those who are born in January and October.

Those who would desire to become true disciples of this Illumined One will need to cast off all that which has out-worn its usefulness, be it a mental attitude, religious outlook, or a way of life. Such individuals must also seek to stimu-late activity within others, through the positive expression of their own understanding of the true purpose of life in the world of matter, demonstrating this within some form of creative activity wherever possible. They should also seek to inspire and lead the weak in spirit along those paths which unaided, they may fear to tread.

The task of the 'One' individual is to become the torch-bearer (in itself a highly occult responsibility) illuminating for others life's tortuous path and identifying the hidden pitfalls thereon, whilst courageously demonstrating their new-found concept for life. They must never, even for one moment of personal doubt, allow the light of truth they carry to be extinguished, thus plunging into the darkness of uncertainty and fear those whom they seek to guide. Such acts create deep karmic ties which may take many lifetimes to eradicate.

The Ascended Master Hilarion appears upon the Fifth Ray of Scientific Thought and will seek to expand the levels of awareness of those subject to this vibration, particularly those whose destiny lies within the exploration of the sciences, both practical and occult. To this end He will utilise the Yellow Ray to stimulate their mental faculties into greater activity.

The Master Hilarion

The Lady Mary

The vibration of the Lady Mary corresponds to that of the Moon, which in turn relates to the feminine principle of the supreme Source of All Life (God.) Those born on the 2nd and the 20th (but *not* those born on the 11th or the 29th) come under the inspirational guidance of the Lady Mary. She will seek to encourage adaptability and co-operation in all walks of life, for all under Her tutelage must learn to blend with their environment, becoming powerful through the virtue of their co-operation.

In addition all who are drawn toward the Lady Mary also need to develop and expand the positive (masculine) aspect of their dual nature, becoming in time the true 'power behind the throne' in their own environment, diverting attention from their true purpose through loving compliance with the demands of others.

Within the age yet to come, it is in the field of sensitivity that the influence of this Illumined One will be most potent. She has inspired humanity throughout the ages, first as the Moon Goddess Ishtar, where she brought Her influence to bear upon the Mesopotamian culture; later in Greece where she was revered as the Goddess Diana, and in modern times as the Virgin Mother of the Master Jesus. The manifestation of the energies of this Illumined One have therefore, long provided a signal for the human race to begin once more the expansion of the feminine aspects of its dual nature. In particular those who are subject to the vibration of the number 2 should make determined efforts to develop their latent mediumistic qualities, taking care to then utilise these for the benefit of humanity.

The Lady Mary

The Venetian Master

The Venetian Master is one of two members of the Masters Lodge who currently combine their efforts to bring about a new point of focus in the related fields of sound and colour. The energies of the Venetian Master are currently being focused upon the task of bringing new pastel shades of colour into being and encouraging their use in creative undertakings. This task involves the splitting of the atoms of the colour rays themselves and must first take place upon the higher Planes of Consciousness, from where they will gradually filter through to this dense Plane of Matter. Therefore, anyone who desires to become a disciple of this Illumined Being should seek to express themselves within these associated fields of endeavour.

Those who are born on the 3rd: 12th: 21st and the 30th, plus those born in March and December can expect the Venetian Master to greatly influence their personal mode of expression during the current life experience. He links with humanity upon the Golden Yellow Ray of the Intellect which, being the Ray of Practical Science and Knowledge, will encourage the expansion of mental power.

Often, those born to experience the 3 vibration gravitate towards the arts, seeking self - expression in colour, artistic form or music, but it is only classical musicians who come under the scrutiny of the Venetian Master. New forms of music (arising from the blending of eastern and western classical styles) will come into being during the New Age and the vibrations arising from these new sounds will usher in the new, softer shades of colour.

The Venetian Master

The Master El Morya

The Master El Morya heads all schools of esoteric thought world-wide and it is His influence which stimulates those who desire to expand their level of self-awareness, to begin to seek active participation within those organisations which endeavour to increase public awareness of the Universal Mind. The Father of the modern-day sciences of numerology and astrology He appears upon the 1st Ray of the Will and all those born on the 4th: 13th: and 31st - but *not* those born on the 22nd, will come under His careful scrutiny.

Currently, the energies of this Master are being focused upon those world leaders who are possessed of a wider vision than most, in an effort to bring about co-operation and mutual tolerance in world situations. He also seeks to reactivate awareness of the Divine Origin of All Life within humanity, encouraging thereby the desire to serve others for the joy it brings about.

He is one of a small group within the Masters Lodge whose energies are largely devoted to paving the way for the New Age, within which He will assume the role of the Manu (or Perfect Man) upon whose characteristics the new race will be developed. To this end He currently endeavours to bring about the elimination of all dogmas and ideologies which have outworn their usefulness and to prepare the way for the new truths which will surface within the Age of Aquarius.

The Master El Morya

The Master Serapis

For those born on the 5th: 14th and 23rd, together with those born in May, the influence of the Master Serapis can aid the expansion of mental activity, for with absolute mastery of thought, the individual can be transformed into a mighty being, fully cognisant of their personal destiny.

In consciously seeking to become His disciple, these individuals will be expected to absorb a deal of responsibility relating to the outgrowth of consciousness within the Kingdom of Nature, developing thereby, a full understanding of, and co-operation with, the Elemental Forces.

Equally, with their mental faculties finely attuned to Planetary Purpose, they will be encouraged to pursue all manner of scientific research, particularly that which is linked to the development of a form of technology employing natural forces which will result in the discovery of new sources of a non-polluting energy.

As this Master appears upon the Violet and Amethyst Rays, His energies are very closely attuned to the New Age of Aquarius and to the esoteric disciplines which will evolve during it. Those responding to His vibration can expect rigorous testing to ascertain their worthiness for occult responsibility, for he also controls initiates of Atlantean and Egyptian temple rituals which are enacted on the Higher Planes of Consciousness at the time of full moon.

Although this Illumined One focuses much of His attention upon the evolution of the Devic / Angelic Kingdom, He also inspires the many artistic and theatrical movements worldwide. A great many of those who incarnate to experience the 5 vibration will be drawn to seek personal expression and (hopefully) expansion within the field of artistic endeavour.

The Master Serapis

The Master Kuthumi

The energies of the Master Kuthumi are exceptionally potent at this time, for He aspires to transform current dogmatic thinking within the Christian faith in order that the true concept of Unconditional Love may manifest. To this end He seeks to influence all who lead or serve within the field of religious expression or education. During the Age of Aquarius He will emerge as the World Teacher, a role He currently shares with The Master Jesus.

All who are born on the 6th: 15th and 24th, together with those born in June will be inspired to reflect upon the necessity to bring about unity within their environment; to come to terms with the truth that all life-forms are inter-dependant and to accept the responsibilites which arise in the area of personal relationships.

This Illumined Being who is an Initiate of the 2nd Ray of Love and Wisdom, is the Doorkeeper of the ancient occult mysteries and also the Co-Protector - along with the Arch-Angel Michael, of the Holy Grail. This ancient mystical quest for total self - awareness has eluded the majority of mankind throughout time. But as the great earth changes which will mark the end of the Piscean Age take place, the Master Kuthumi will provide the key to this inner search, by reactivating long-lost knowledge.

The six - pointed star reflects the energy of the Master Kuthumi, symbolising perfect equilibrium, for within the number 6 all forces unite. Those who aspire to follow this Radiant Being will be required to demonstrate perfect balance on all fronts, loving all life-forms in an unconditional manner, whilst seeking perfection upon the inner path of self-awareness.

The Master Kuthumi

This illustration represents the powers of the Master Kuthumi, activating the Higher Consciousness of Mankind.

All who are born on the 6th: 15th: and 24th are guided by the Master Kuthumi to reflect upon the necessity for unity within all that which they undertake; to come to terms with the truth that all life-forms are interdependant and that they must therefore be prepared to shoulder many great responsibilites during their current life experience.

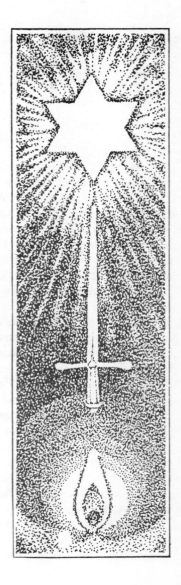

Illustration by Ann Becker.

The Master Rakoczy

The energy of this Illumined One manifests upon the 7th Ray of Ritual and Ceremony and He is identified by the Violet Flame of which he is Lord. Known as the Regent of Europe, He enjoys a more popular appeal than the majority of those within the Masters' Lodge largely because He has closely identified Himself with the outgrowth of consciousness, particularly within Europe where He is perhaps better known as The Comte de St.Germain.

In co-operation with the Venetian Master He works to improve the quality of life world - wide, through the perfecting of the sounds we currently utilise in our everyday lives. Although His energies have been largely focused in the Western Hemisphere during the past three centuries, this is shortly to change as He seeks to develop new and more harmonious sounds in the field of musical expression, particularly in the East. By and large, the human race creates its own environment and we are greatly influenced by the many discordant vibrations we set in motion within it. New, more melodic sounds will, together with gentler pastel hues of colour, lead to a more positive lifestyle, ensuring thereby a greater measure of growth and expansion of consciousness.

In a former lifetime this Master was known as Lao Tse the great Eastern Mystic, and according to one of His pupils He stated that 'the perfect man employs his mind as a mirror. It grasps nothing. It refuses nothing. It receives but does not retain. Thus he can triumph over matter without injury to himself.' A perfect description of the lesson which the number 7 has to teach us all.

All who are born on the 7th: 16th: and the 25th, together with those born in July come under the scrutiny of this Master, who will encourage the inward focus of their energies, in a bid to establish communication with the Higher Self. In turn this will lead to the activation of the Higher Senses, establishing a link with the non - physical Planes of Consciousness, the outcome of which can be a fount of inspirational guidance.

The Master Rakoczy

The Lord Maitreya

The Lord Maitreya is the Over-Lord or Over-seer for our solar system and He operates from the Higher Ethers from where He seeks to raise the level of consciousness within all of humanity. In the past He focused His energies through the agency of different Masters and World Teachers at times of world need but, despite this fact, He is not concerned with individual consciousness, but with that of the masses.

His vibration of colour is that of pure white light which even today is being radiated within the atmosphere of the earth. This intense light is assimilated by the human race through the Etheric Body, where it is then transformed into a living energy which serves to sustain us within this Plane of Matter.

The Lord Maitreya is not the Logos for the planet Earth but serves as its Over-Lord ensuring the continuation of all life forms, not only upon the Earth but also upon other planets within our solar system.

Currently he influences all who are involved in the field of physics or scientific research, encouraging them to expand their consciousness beyond the intellectual level. During their nightly 'out-of-body' journeys these individuals have the opportunity to tap into vast sources of knowledge which, if brought back to the waking state, could greatly benefit the human race.

Those born on the 8th: 17th: and 26th: plus those born in August particularly draw the attention of this Illumined Soul, who will observe their reactions to the many situations of restraint to which they will be subject. Only through the conscious acceptance of the inevitable will these individuals reach the stage of initiation they have incarnated to attain.

The Lord Maitreya

The Master Jesus

Those who are born on the 9th: 18th: and the 27th, together with those born in September are inspired by the Master Jesus to seek attainment of a goal set in motion during an earlier life experience, whereby, through a life spent in loving and unconditional service to humanity, they may achieve the measure of growth necessary to free themselves from the bonds of matter.

Being a 6th Ray Master, this Illumined One will stimulate devotion within His disciples or activate a desire to follow an indealistic path through life, and those so influenced by Him will begin to long for a personal link or contact. Through the field of devoted and selfless service to those less fortunate than themselves they may well attain this one day.

In common with the Lord Maitreya whom He loyally serves, the Master Jesus focuses His attention and energies on the mass of humaity rather than upon certain individuals. His point of focus is modern-day Christianity and in particular those who worship within the Christian faith, whose minds He seeks to prepare for the coming of the new World Teacher during the Aquarian Age. (A role that is to be played by the Master Kuthumi.)

During two physical incarnations this Illumined One made the supreme sacrifice and served as the conscious vehicle (or channel) for the Lord Maitreya, and together they now seek to advance awareness within all of humanity of the need for self-discipline and the acceptance of personal responsibility for all thought and action. This in turn can lead to Self Realisation or God Consciousness.

Those drawn toward service in the various forms of healing expression can be assured of the interest of this Master, particularly where time is spent in assisting the afflicted to overcome their state of disharmony through the constructive use of thought.

The Master Jesus

The Lady Nada

The Lady Nada links with the highest of ideals in mankind, stimulating pure thought in those who come under Her influence, inspiring action undertaken with the purest of intent. She represents the highest pinnacle it is possible for the aspirant to achieve in the field of idealistic endeavour, but along the path toward success lie many pitfalls, not the least of which is illusion. The rallying cry of all who seek to follow the inspiration of the Lady Nada should be 'try, try and try again!' for they have incarnated to experience some rather bitter disappointments, as their idealistic propositions are constantly rejected as unworkable by those around and about them.

Those who are born on the 11th and the 29th, together with born in November come under the influence of this Illumined One. In some schools of thought the number 11 is reduced to 2, which serves to identify the feminine principle in our dual natures. Although this aspect of the self will be very evident in those born to experience the 11 vibration, their lessons will be much more arduous, with emphasis being placed upon the practical expression of all idealistic concepts.

The Lady Nada appears upon the Seventh Ray of Ritual and Ceremony which will be the predominant Ray within Western Europe during the coming Age of Aquarius and those who aspire to follow Her example must be prepared to tend to the needs of both planet and humanity. A major task for these individuals lies within the conscious development of their intuitive capacities, to the extent where it can be said of them that 'they walk with Angels and men' - hence the earlier warning on illusion.

Upon Her brow this Illumined One wears a faceted Amethyst gemstone which represents the colour ray upon which She manifests. This in itself reflects the purest aspect of the Violet Ray, and serves to illustrate the path on which many of this Adept's energies will be focused. Currently Lady Nada seeks to expand awareness of the various healing energies and to encourage participation by Her disciples in this field of loving endeavour. Today many ancient healing techniques are being reactivated, largely in a bid to aid mankind overcome the disharmony which arises from the abuse of thought. All born to experience the 11 vibration will themselves be expected to master this potent force and demonstrate, in a thoroughly practical manner, just how others may achieve the same goal.

The Lady Nada

The Master Djwal Khul

The accompanying portrait may come as quite a surprise to those who are accustomed to that which currently circulates within some esoteric groups, for it differs greatly from that illustration. However this Master considers Himself to be the youngest (in terms of experience no doubt) within the Masters' Lodge, being the most recent among their number to undertake the Fifth Initiation.

All of the illustrations shown within these pages are inspired by the thought patterns of the Masters themselves, who state that they are in a sense illusionary, in that they no longer hold physical or etheric forms. (Or for that matter, any form that mankind could recognise as relating to the physical realm.) These illustrations therefore serve to depict the particular energy patterns of certain members of the Masters Lodge, captured by an extremely gifted and sensitive channel and provided by the Masters for their potential disciples, in a bid to satisfy their desire for a visual focal point.

The Master Djwal Khul is a 2nd Ray Master who works very closely with the Master Kuthumi; indeed He is one of the Brothers of the Golden Robe, of which Kuthumi is Hierarch. Currently His labours involve Him in the instruction of many pupils of the various Masters who can benefit from His knowledge for He, more than any other member of the Masters Lodge, has a vast knowledge of the energies and the effects of the different rays which so influence humanity.

For those born on the 22nd the energies of this Illumined One provide a perfect balance, as He appears upon the Emerald Green Ray and further emphasises this aspect of harmony with three large emeralds, signifying that balance is to be achieved through positive self expression.

Master Djwal Khul concentrates His energies upon those who serve within the various forms of healing endeavour (particularly those who serve in an altruistic manner) and those '22' individuals who follow similar paths will receive a great deal of His attention, as will those who seek to express their idealism in a thoroughly practical manner within the various welfare organisations worldwide, or in philanthropic movements such as the Red Cross.

The Master Djwal Khul

Birthday Synopsis

Whilst each numeric vibration has a particular lesson to teach all those who are subject to it, some vibrations are more intense than others ie: those born on the 10th will be subject to greater stress than those who are born on the 1st, largely due to the addition of the naught. Whereas the '1' person comes under the scrutiny of the Master Hilarion, the person born on the 10th will also be subject to the attention of the Maha Chohan. This will lead to greater demands being made upon them and they will be expected to outstrip a '1' person in any given undertaking. This law applies equally to those who are born on the 20th and the 30th.

I will deal with the specific lessons attached to each vibration in the following chapters, but here I endeavour to provide an 'at a glance' synopsis of the major lessons to be mastered by those born on the various days of the month.

1st : Those who are born on the 1st need to learn to take the lead in a positive manner whilst avoiding excessive use of the will in a bid to subdue those subject to their authority. Some who experience this vibration tend to shy away from responsibility, even to the point of becoming recluses. Such action should be avoided at all costs, for the lesson here is *Independence* and those born on the 1st have to avoid becoming dependent upon others. Above all, they have to learn to demonstrate the positive (or masculine) aspects of their nature within a highly original approach toward life.

2nd: All '2' individuals tend to respond in a highly emotional manner to everyday situations and wherever possible should avoid the tendency to stubbornly refuse to comply with the demands of others, for this will only bring about greater suffering. As they tend to be extremely sensitive individuals, they should endeavour to develop this 'feminine' side of their dual nature, for it can assist them in the task of *adapting* to life's constantly changing situations.

3rd : Herein lies a golden opportunity for the expansion of the *Personality* , whereby the individual may attain growth through Self Expression in creative undertakings. Although social gatherings will result in a great deal of personal popularity, the '3' individuals should avoid flitting from blossom to blossom or experience to experience, lest they lose out overall, for this could lead to the development of a cyncial outlook on life.

4th: The willpower is to the fore in those who incarnate to experience this vibration and the correct use of this powerful force is their major lesson in life. '4' individuals can prove to be somewhat forceful characters who invariably seek to dominate others and learn to their cost, that such actions bring unhappiness and loneliness in their wake. They should also avoid rebellion without just cause, learning instead to rejoice in the many opportunities which life will present wherein they might demonstrate a measure of personal responsibility combined with a *practical* approach toward life. The ' 4 ' person should also be prepared to work extremely hard for whatever they desire in life, accepting the many necessary limitations which will ensure that their energies are ever harnessed to practicality.

5th: The control of all thought, speech and action is vital to ensure success - therefore, butterfly mind be still! Although restless by nature, '5' individuals should endeavour to develop that almost magical quality they possess for *communication* within the many opportunities which will be presented to them, whilst seeking to demonstrate the various creative facets of their highly complex natures. They should endeavour to control any tendency to waste their lives in sensual or illusionary pursuits or in side - stepping responsibility.

6th: These individuals must beware the many pitfalls

that lie ahead of them on the emotional level for they incarnate to demonstrate an ability to rise above the carnal nature, but may well experience a measure of difficulty in this direction. Their goal lies within the reflection of caring, *unconditional love* for all of humanity, never being deterred or hurt when this love is not returned. Equally they need to accept the many responsibilites which will arise within their relationships during the present incarnation.

7th: Here we find those who are deeply sensitive - natural psychics who must beware vain illusion (the trap which will ever seek to ensnare them.) Due to their extreme sensitivity many will desire to flee the cities and towns in favour of the peace and tranquility of the countryside, the calming energies of which can assist with the balancing of their delicate natures.

Although such breathing spaces may well prove to be necessary from time to time, '7' individuals should always bear in mind that their life purpose lies in providing positive and constructive direction for all in need and that they must not sever all contact with the world at large. Overall they need to come to terms with the *psychic* and psychological aspects of their highly complex natures and locate some method of developing their powerful mental capacities, possibly along scientific lines.

8th: For those who experience this vibration, opposition, conflicts and restriction will abound, largely serving to encourage the freeing of the self from the vain illusions of this world of matter, whilst stimulating the ability to rise above the mundane. The lesson here is relatively simple - learn to *accept the inevitable* and so overcome all adversity. Although these individuals are inclined to pursue power and monetary gain, the many testing situations which will arise throughout their lifetime will eventually lead them toward an inner awareness of the illusionary quality of material riches and success.

9th: A choice exists for those whose lesson this is: a full and satisfying life devoted to *selfless service* to mankind or one of selfish self-indulgence. The choice lies between growth and stagnation. Where the former is selected, care should be taken not to over - extend the self in good works for such activity will prevent them from undertaking other tasks which lie around the corner. The vibration of the number 9 provides those who are subject to it with an opportunity to bring to fruition the ambition of an earlier life experience. To ignore the opportunities for growth within *universal service* is to fail self.

10th: The energy of the number '1' is heightened here, the addition of the '0' serving to intensify both the positive and the negative characteristics of those subject to it and the warning attendant to the '1' vibration should be carefully noted. Those born on the 10th possess excellent mental capacities, which if fully developed can lead to positive achievement, but they should take care not to dominate others in the pursuit of personal objectives.

The '10' individual may act with a flourish but the minor details often elude them, so whatever task they undertake in life must clearly bear their stamp of originality. Natural leaders, they should be prepared to shoulder many responsibilites in life, leading others through the power of their example.

11th: Here we locate the dreamers of this world, full of high, fine ideals but all too often lacking in *practicality*. The '11' individuals will often be deeply hurt by those they encounter in daily life due to the rejection of their high standards and *idealistic* outlook, and will need to learn to express those ideals in a thoroughly down to earth and practical manner. Above all, these people must overcome the tendency to retreat to cloud nine and from there to fire thunderbolts toward those who dared to disagree.

12th: Encouraging a tendency to enjoy life to the full, the planet Jupiter (which influences this vibration) will also impel those who are subject to it toward social gatherings and lighthearted affairs. Despite this, these individuals should not overlook the many valuable opportunities which will be presented, wherein a measure of self - expression may be attained.

On a secondary level, the Sun and the Moon join forces to create confusion within the self and although the Sun does provide the stronger influence, encouraging personal independence, these individuals should ensure that the emotional aspect of their nature does not prevent expression of their natural leadership qualities, particularly within creative undertakings. However, cynicism and the lower emotional nature could well win the day here.

13th: Luck is relative - and very much a state of the mind. If all those who are born on the 13th will only keep their minds firmly fixed upon the task in hand (with all minor details noted) accidents cannot occur. The Sun's influence will encourage the development of leadership qualities in unusual and creative ways, but these individuals must always be aware of the power of their will, making certain that they do not abuse this potent force, for they could well live to rue the day. Practicality of approach on all levels and the necessity to complete all tasks commenced, should be the aim of all who experience this particular vibration, overcoming thereby the accident - prone image which so many '13' individuals project.

14th: Those born to experience this vibration could fall into one of two categories: either strong-willed leaders or weak-willed shirkers whose ability to have the last word will often leave the opposition gasping - invariably due to its critical tone. Major lessons needing to be absorbed lie within the total control of the thought patterns, postive application of the will - power and the use of the critical faculty in a totally constructive manner.

15th: Gifted with silver tongues and motivated by a desire to take the lead, these individuals could emerge at the head of organisations whose energies are devoted to answering human need, for they will be stimulated by a desire to love and be loved. The latter could well plunge them into many a difficult situation, for suspicion and jealousy may never be far below the surface. These negative traits will have to be mastered if they are to establish a lasting relationship. Those born on the 15th are possessed of highly emotional and changeable natures and they should ever be on guard against despondency which can arise when opposition is encountered in life.

16th: Those who incarnate to undergo this lesson in sensitivity can expect to experience a certain amount of despair, unless they can curb their readiness to accept everyone at face value. Should they choose to ignore this warning (preferring to follow their emotional responses) they will only reap disappointment until they learn to utilise their intuitive ability to identify illusion. Despite their innate sensitivity, the '16' individual has to learn to develop strength of character, being positive in thought and deed when all about them are in despair. As *llusion* is the keynote of this vibration, many will tend to expend their energies in illusionary pursuits, with the emotions well to the fore.

17th: A great many testing situations lie before those born on this day but their innate sensitivity, coupled with determination to overcome all opposition, could well make this a lifetime of positive achievment. Failure lies within negative responses to such tests and blank refusal to co-operate on any level with others. Acceptance of that which is patently inevitable will aid development of inner strengths and ensure success, either in the business world or the field of spiritual endeavour.

18th: The Sun and Saturn combine to test the resolve of these individuals to serve humanity, despite tremendous opposition. They have to learn to control their explosive Martian temperament, refusing to give way to the frustrations which are likely to arise, due to the many obstacles they will encounter in seeking to satisfy personal desire. There is a great potential for spiritual growth upon this vibration, always provided that the individual concerned can avoid the development of a selfish or resentful mode of thought.

19th: For those born to experience this vibration life is what they are prepared to make of it, for extremely powerful forces influence all actions undertaken during this lifetime, the influence of the Sun and Mars providing them with the potential for dynamic leadership, particularly in the field of universal service.

On the lower side of this vibration, those subject to it who refuse to play their part in the game of life, may well experience a somewhat empty existence, one without much leavening. There is the indication of karmic patterns working out with this number, stemming largely from the misuse of power in former life experiences.

20th: Those born on this day tend to react in a rather intense manner, particularly where emotional encounters are concerned, for they are extremely sensitive to the reactions of those around and about them and should learn to control any tendency toward depression. Where possible, they should set aside all personal ambition and desires and involve themselves in groups, partnerships or family life, where they may put to use their natural diplomatic skills, bringing about harmony.

21st: The influence of the planet Jupiter is revealed in the friendly and likeable natures of those born on the 21st and they should seize all opportunities presented to express their imaginative powers in an artistic or creative manner. How - ever, on a secondary level the influence of the Moon predominates, stimulating emotional responses whilst the Sun encourages the will to succeed in those difficult situations which demand total adaptability and positive expression.

22nd: A tendency to 'sit on the fence' is a characteristic of many born on the 22nd, for this is one of the most difficult of vibrations to master and for the majority this may well prove to be a somewhat stressful lifetime. As a result, the emotions may well be to the fore coupled with a rebellious will. Despite the many conflicting demands that will be made of them, these individuals need to become balanced in their outlook and to remain calm in the midst of conflict, utilising their intuitive powers to produce constructive benefits for humanity.

23rd: Often restless individuals, those who are born on this day may not find this to be a particularly easy life experience, largely due to their mercurial nature and a tendency to respond in an emotional manner to restrictive situations. They may also prove to be great procrastinators. However, as they are gifted with quick minds they can easily ovecome day-to-day difficulties. Beset by a need for frequent change and constantly fired with the urge to travel, these individuals will find that short journeys can easily satisfy the wanderlust without disrupting daily life. Invariably talented, these individuals should attempt to present their highly original ideas in an entertaining manner to ensure success.

24th: The major lesson which those born on the 24th have to master is the conquering of the lower nature, transmuting sensual desires into unconditional love for all of mankind. This may be achieved by the channelling of the emotional nature into some form of selfless service. Failure may eventuate if time and energy are mis-spent in sensual pursuits. Possessing a conscientous nature, this is best expressed in those situations which require a sympathetic response to those in need and the acceptance of all responsibilities which arise during the course of relationships.

25th: Here we locate the natural psychic, gifted in the field of 'other-world' communication - someone who must at all costs, avoid becoming emotionally involved in the problems of those they endeavour to assist. Those born on this day are often highly sensitive individuals who have a tendecy to be emotional, moody and somewhat mercurial in their responses. Their life lesson includes the need to adapt to their environment and to subdue any tendency toward self-centred activities. The area of personal relationships may well prove to be a minefield, due to their inability to respond to love or to share this with others.

26th: The combined influence of the Moon and the planet Venus upon those born on this day may well result in highly emotional responses to the many situations of restraint these individuals will be expected to endure. Determined efforts to accept that which is patently inevitable have to be made throughout the lifetime, if they are to achieve any measure of success with this vibration. Where their response to opposition is bitterness or stubborn resentment, they will retard their spiritual progress (and set in motion painful health conditions). Most born on this day do have a capacity to excel in the business and financial spheres , possessing strong managerial abilities. Despite their reserved natures, these individuals can be quite affectionate.

27th: Here we find powerful Martian energies channelled through rather complex minds and sensitive natures. The key to this lifetime lies in selfless service to humanity, within which emotional entanglements have to be avoided. The development of their intuitive ability would serve to guide them their steps through life. These individuals should endeavour to keep the Martian impulse firmly under control, avoiding temperamental outbursts or draining their energy levels in physical undertakings - to the detriment of their health.

28th: Many obstacles and petty restrictions will be encountered throughout this lifetime by those who are subject to this vibration and they must learn to discern their purpose, avoiding the tendency to respond in an emotional manner. Equally, much responsibility will come their way and this should be willingly shouldered and not pushed aside. The influence of the Moon and Saturn may well create all manner of difficulties for these individuals who need to learn to reflect the innate vitality and leadership qualities which the Sun bestows upon them. Above all, they must press on regardless, bearing in mind the fact that all of the world loves a winner!

29th: For those born on this day, their spiritual ideals and desire to aid all of humanity will all too often be overshadowed by their emotional responses to the rejection of their dreams by others. At all costs they should endeavour to avoid the tendency to become dreamers, seeking instead to develop a completely natural approach toward life. Gifted as visionarys, these individuals should seek some form of humanitarian service in which they might utilise their insight.

30th: The influence of the planet Jupiter will assist

those born on this day to express themselves in the field of entertainment or that of the arts, for the development of their creative capacities is vital during the current lifetime. Possessed of warm, friendly and outgoing natures these individuals usually become cherished companions, someone whose presence is greatly sought after. They should however, try to avoid becoming absorbed in trivia and to curb a natural tendency to be easily bored and restless. If success is desired they need to focus all energys upon one task at a time.

31st: Self expression in the field of leadership is possible for all born on this day, largely due to the combined influence of the planet Jupiter and the Sun. However they will need to avoid excessive use of their powerful wills in a bid to gain their own ends, learning instead to lead by the power of their example. If they are to achieve a measure of success in life, practicality must also be developed and all limitation encountered in daily life accepted as a vital necessity. Invariably possessing rather serious natures, these individuals often shun social life and learn to their cost that a stubborn nature and a rigid attitude invariably lead to great unhappiness.

Positive Attributes and Negative Traits

Every numerical vibration has a specific lesson to teach those who are subject to its influence. In addition to its positive aspect, each vibration also has a negative side to it and unless forewarned, many fail to achieve their intended goal in life, due to their tendency to follow the line of least resistance.

Take for example the number 1. The goal of those subject to this vibration is to seek independance, the influence of the Sun which rules it, stimulating leadership qualities. Few among their number will have sufficient strength of character to reflect this aspect of the vibration and may tend toward submission to the wills of others, servitude, or total inaction. They could equally develop an autocratic or authoritarian manner, seeking to dominate weaker-willed individuals.

Study the positive and negative traits which are indicated under each number in order to understand the self and then to assist others to know themselves.

No.	Positive Attributes.	Negative Traits.
1	Independence: Courage: Pioneering impulse: Individuality: Self confidence: Ambition: Perseverance:	Introversion: Idleness: Dependency: Egotism: Agression: Dictatorial: Stubbornness: Non-co-operation: Intolerance:

No.	Positive Attributes.	Negative Traits.
2	Adaptability: Tact: Diplomacy: Charm: Co-operative: Ability to develop the ideas of others:	Oversensitive: Fearful: Emotional instability: Melancholia: Stubborn: Weak character: Superficial in outlook:
3	Artisitic: Creative: Linguistic: Optimistic: Sociability: Enthusiastic:	Conceit: Procrastination Extravagance:Worrying Cynical: Exaggeration: Inarticulate: Tendency to diffuse energies:
4	Ability to organise: Practicality: Efficiency: Tenacity: Responsible: Systematic:	Inattentive: Rebellious: Domineering: Cruelty: Impatient: Careless: Resistance to change: Impracticality:
5	Lucidity of thought: Ability to inspire others: Artisitic creativity: Ability to communicate: Teaching capacity:	Destructive thinking: Avoiding responsibility Lack of staying power: Restless: Pessimistic: Deceitful:
6	Loyalty: Sympathy: Responsible: Sociability: Benevolence: Loving: Harmonious:	Argumentative: Interfering: Anxiety: Irresponsibility in close relationships: Jealousy: 'Poor me' syndrome:

No.	Positive Attributes	Negative Traits
7	Psychic ability: Religious outlook: Introspective: Perfectionist: Modesty:	Hypersensitivity: Over-emotional:Moody Inferiority complex: Melancholia: Critical: Delusionary
8	Ambition: Practicality: Analytical mind: Impersonal judgment: Business-like manner: Self-controlled:	Intolerance:Impatience: Ruthless in opposition: Pride: Fear: Tyranical: Weak willed: Miserly: Resentful:
9	Desire to serve others: Compassionate: Philanthropic:	Selfishness: Aggression Self-focussed: Temperamental:
11	Extreme sensitivity: Idealistic: Honesty: Practical: Helpful:	Impracticality: Fanaticism: Aimless: Obstinacy: Despairing; Day-dreaming:
22	Humanitarian outlook: Perceptive: Balanced outlook: Leadership qualities:	Instability: Boastful: Recklessness: Inferiority complex: Self-centred:

Getting To Know Yourself

There are three numerical vibrations which could be said to reflect that which we are. These are:

The Governing Factor, found within the **Day of Birth**:

The Destiny Factor, represented by the sum total of entire **Date of Birth**: and finally the

Overall Self Expression, located in the sum total of the vibrations found within the **Given Names** we bear.

The first of these, the Governing Factor, indicates the manner in which individuals will react to given situations, whilst striving to locate opportunities wherein they might express the finer elements of their natures - represented by the Destiny Factor, which is the *overall* goal in life.

Nonetheless, we may at times express ourselves in a manner seemingly at odds with our major life lessons, for we are also sub ject to the influence of the numeric vibrations found within our given names, and this can lead to a deal of inner conflict. Equally, in situations where the *Destiny Factor* and the *Overall Self Expression* lines carry the same lesson, there may be a tendency to respond in a somewhat negative manner to many situations, for this duplication of lessons indicates a failure to master this vibration during an earlier life experience.

All other lessons, no matter where encountered, be they primary or secondary, serve to highlight these three major vibrations. There is nothing haphazard in creation, all lines of expression being very carefully laid down prior to incarnation, to ensure that we may locate and achieve our true purpose in life.

As the first twenty-eight years of every lifetime are invariably spent in tying up the loose ends from an earlier life experience, much that occurs during this period cannot be sidestepped. The *Governing Factor* lesson which influences this initial phase of the lifetime serves to indicate the positive qualities each individual should seek to develop.

Success on this level will only come about once we learn to act in a responsible manner and to accept the necessity for certain obstacles or difficulties. These in themselves serve to test our determination to attain the greater goal in life - that which is indicated by the *Destiny Factor* lesson.

Taking these lessons one step at a time, let us consider the date of birth shown below in a bid to identify the various lessons therein. First set out the date of birth and then reduce each segment to a single digit, commencing with the Day of Birth. Simply add the 1 to the 2, revealing the *Governing Factor* of 3.

	12th	June	1963		
This reduces to:	3	6	(19) = 1	= 1.

Governing Factor = 3 = Self Expression and Expansion.

To identify the *Personality Factor* lesson apply a numeric energy to the month of birth (June being the sixth month), and finally, the *Maturity Factor* lesson lies hidden within the numbers which make up the year of birth. Add these together; the 1 to the 9 to make 10, plus 6 making 16 and then the 3 to reach a total of 19. (However as 19 is a Danger Signal vibration it must be highlighted in the chart before reducing to a single digit). Add the 1 to the 9 to make 10 and then further reduce this to 1. Complete this task by adding all of the sub-totals together in order to arrive at the *Destiny Factor* - which amounts to 1.

The primary lesson for this person lies within the necessity to express themselves in day-to-day undertakings, whereby he or she may develop as a personality. This expression may be found in the field of the arts, through music, the use of colour or the creative use of the hands, say as a sculptor or in carpentry. It could equally be found on the home-front (particularly in this case, where the Personality Factor lesson influencing mid-life indicates a need to love others in an unconditional manner).

As this formative phase of the life will be greatly influenced by the planet Jupiter, there may well be a tendency to fritter time and energies in social undertakings, for this is intended to be an enjoyable lifetime - and those subject to the influence of this vibration rarely overlook an opportunity to do so.

Care must be taken to ensure that the negative aspect of this vibration does not predominate, for it could lead to the development of a cynical attitude to life or in an extreme reluctance to participate in social events.

Study the lessons attendant to each and every one of the Governing Factor vibrations and then put the knowledge so gained into practice on the following Work Space.

Work Space

Date of Birth:

Reducing to:

Governing Factor:

Conclusions:

Date of Birth:

Reducing to:

Governing Factor:

Conclusions:

One

Governing those born on the 1st: 10th:19th: & 28th

Here souls enter the world of matter in a bid to experience all that which such worlds may teach it. The major lesson with this particular vibration is to develop individual-istic attributes, thereby identifying themselves to the mass of humanity. The emphasis here is to achieve **Independence** rather than be dependant upon the strength of others. If this can be attained it will lead them to focus attention upon their capacity for leadership and the super-vision of others, achieved at all times via the power of their own example.

To this end many situations will offer responsibilities which the 'One' individual should willingly shoulder. Although this vibration reflects all that is considered masculine, all too often this task falls to the women of our world who courageously accept the burden of family care and support.

With the Master Hilarion influencing thought and action at the higher level, those born on this day will be led to seek expression in new and unusual ways, and the sciences (both practical and occult) may hold a strong fascination. The Sun is the ruling planet here bringing great warmth to the personality, stimulating positive action on many fronts, reflecting as it does, all of the masculine characteristics of the Father/Mother God.

The influence of the number One can be seen at work within the ambitions of most individuals, providing the impetus, assisting the inventive, and stimulating pioneering impulses. Indeed the energy of the number One can be noted in positive activities of all kinds. However, there are ever two options open to all of mankind and all too often we tend to take the line of least resistance, thereby negating what may well have been positive attainments.

Those born to experience this vibration should be ever watchful for latent tendencies toward laziness or of becoming mulish in the face of opposition. They should also avoid developing a dictatorial manner when placed in a situation of authority, or side-stepping responsibility when presented. They should also endeavour to prevent the formation of unnecessary fears, which can lead to imbalance - and ill-health.

Two

Governing those born on the 2nd and the 20th

Upon this illusionary Plane of Matter, the Moon greatly influences the emotional responses of mankind. Those incarnate to master the Two vibration will be hard pressed at times to maintain a natural equilibrium, as the Moon governs this vibration. The stimulus of the lunar energy activates the feminine principle of our dual natures and, like the Moon itself, these individuals will need to learn to reflect the positive or masculine apsects of their natures.

Moon children will ever be expected to adapt to the desires and needs of those around and about them and must seek to place these before the desires of the self. Indeed, should they fail to adapt to the constantly changing tides of opinion and those situations which arise from them, they may well suffer rejection, which will in turn bring about emotional upheaval.

The necessity to become the **Diplomat** will become evident relatively early in life. The silver tongues with which they appear to be blessed may eventually turn many a situation to their advantage for, in appearing to comply with often outrageous suggestions, they dull the suspicions of their adversaries.

They should then wait for the right opportunity wherein the tide may be turned in their favour. Quite often tactful suggestions (after the event) will be readily accepted when it becomes evident that the original, ill-timed decision was perhaps unwise. It is only as an integral part of a group, association or family unit that the 'Two' individuals will locate the measure of growth they require.

On the reverse side of this vibration we encounter those who, because of their senstive natures, tend to be rather shy and who invariably withdraw into the background, fearful of adverse comment or action. Despite this, emotional fires smoulder beneath the surface ignited by apparent injustice. These can at times flare up into angry outbursts and on such occasions the passions are often beyond control.

There may also be a great amount of carlessness evident in the everyday actions of these individuals who may have a tendency toward vacillation. Also, due to the continual changes forced upon them, some 'Two' individuals may consciously seek to deceive in an endeavour to thwart an unwelcome course of action.

This is a very difficult vibration to master, but one which has to be experienced, for it reflects the karma incurred in an earlier lifetime when the needs of others were swept aside or ignored. This time the boot is on another's foot and no matter how unpleasant or irksome certain situations may be, the 'Two' individual should endeavour to adapt to the dictates of others.

The influence of the Lady Mary will be strongly felt by those seeking to express themselves on this vibration, the gentleness of Her outward appearance masking the core of steel within (which all 'Two' individuals should endeavour to emulate). All Moon children are possessed of an innate sensitivity and the development of this quality is vital for it will aid them to communicate with the non-physical Planes of Consciousness. However, due to their fear of the unknown - and of adverse criticism - many will hold back from such a course of action.

Three

Governing those born on the 3rd: 12th: 21st & 30th:

Having mastered the influence of the Sun and the Moon, the slowly developing soul must next endeavour to expand its horizons by developing one or more of its latent talents. For 'Three' individuals a measure of personal growth can be attained by expressing their undoubted abilities in some creative manner, through an ingenious use of colour, in the world of music and dance or in other creative undertakings. For some among their number their greatest personal expression will take place on the home front via the creation of an harmonious environment.

Those who are subject to this vibration will find it to be one that is relatively easy to adapt to, for the influence of Jupiter (which rules this vibration) is said to bring good fortune in its wake. Many 'Three' people will be more than content to enjoy 'the good life' which eventuates, putting off any difficult decisions for another day.

Such responses can lead to the formation of habits which will be difficult to break and these can lead to the wasteful extravagance of time, energy or financial resources. Petty jealousies, intolerance of others' points of view and a tendency to gossip, also reflect the negative aspect of this vibration, as do deceit and a pessimistic outlook on life.

The major lesson the number Three has to teach is the need to balance the desires of the Lower Self (personality) with the needs of the Higher Self (the soul). Those subject to it should endeavour to express in a down-to-earth and practical manner the intuitive direction which they will receive from time to time, for this could well prove to be a much needed lifeline for those who are in despair.

Paulo Veronese, the Venetian Master, oversees the development of those who respond in a positive manner to the higher aspect of this vibration, encouraging an upward shift in their level of consciousness. He will also stimulate interest in the creative use of colour and music, particularly in those who are drawn to seek expression within the healing arts.

Four

Governing those born on the 4th: 13th: & 31st.

A very strong will is evident in those born to experience this vibration, influenced as they are by Uranus the Planet of the Will. These individuals will need to exercise great care when utilising this potent force and no matter what difficulties or opposition they encounter during the course of their life must endeavour to meet these with patient fortitude. However, patience may be a virtue they sadly lack. Furthermore, they will need to demonstrate to all and sundry their capacity to shoulder responsibility and in so doing, their inherent honesty and practicality of purpose must also be clearly visible.

With such a strong will 'Four' people are natural organisers (invariably of others) and some of their number have a streak of cruelty in their natures which may verge on violence when their will is opposed. Unless they can learn to lead by the power of their example many of their undertakings may come to grief. Any tendency to dominate or to over-ride the wishes of others should be firmly controlled.

Due to their narrow and shortsighted outlook upon life these individuals often restrict themselves to a life with little leavening, considering social activity to be without purpose. If there is to be any measure of joy in this life they will need to soften this rather rigid outlook. Although there will be limitations placed upon them during the course of the current lifetime, all 'Four' individuals will need to accept these as a necessary adjunct to life and not respond in a resentful manner.

Sadly, a great many who incarnate to experience this

vibration are rebellious by nature, they reject society's rules and standards perceiving them to be an obstruction to their personal liberty. In extreme cases this can develop into a hatred of authority which will greatly mar their lives.

The influence of the Master El Morya will encourage the constructive use of the willpower, stimulating practical achievement - for all who aspire to follow in the steps of this Illumined One will be required to demonstrate a tolerance for the weaknesses of human nature and to assist those who suffer as the result of such frailties. In this manner they might gradually move toward becoming Initiates of the Will.

Five

Governing those born on the 5th: 14th: & 23rd

Those incarnating to experience this vibration are provided with many opportunities for personal expression obtaining this in diverse ways. Possessed of strong mental powers they have persuasive tongues, likeable personalities and tend to be popular, becoming the centre of attention at any gathering. In any discussion or argument they are determined to have the last word.

Do not try to tie these individuals down as they need to fly free, loving constant change and travel, ever ready to follow the spirit of adventure. Their movements will be swift, reflecting the Mercurial influence, their hands dextrous (as they are invariably creative people). They are extremely versatile, but may often be given to sexual proclivity.

The major lesson for all 'Five' individuals lies in the mastery of their thought and speech (for thoughts are the building blocks of future experience) learning to utilise these in a constructive manner. However many simply follow the free wheeling influence of the planet Mercury which governs this vibration and flit from situation to situation with little intention of coming to grips with responsibility. Nonetheless they have incarnated in a bid to reach an understanding of the freedom they will experience during the current lifetime and to seek an outlet for their diverse talents.

Being natural 'escape artists' these people should avoid the use of alchohol and narcotics to which they can easily become addicted. There may also be a tendency to be thoughtless, irresponsible, and to procrastinate when responding to the lower aspect of this vibration. But with their thoughts firmly under control and their desire for change positively channelled they can become the most positive teachers, fluent speakers and, at times, plausible politicians. Many among them emerge to the fore in the field of entertainment.

The Master Serapis appears on the Air Element and His vibration is perfectly suited to stimulate the average 'Five' person. He will stir them into action both mentally and physically, whilst encouraging the conscious desire to expand their level of consciousness. This may only be attained if they are prepared to exact of themselves a strict measure of self-discipline, particularly in the realm of desire. As His sphere of influence lies within the esoteric and practical sciences together with the use of sound and colour, those who are seriously determined to follow where He leads, will find themselves propelled toward some form of activity in these fields.

Six

Governing those born on the 6th: 15th & 24th:

The major lesson which the six vibration has to teach is that of love. Not the sensual, possessive or corrosive emotion that the majority assume to be love, but the glorious, uplifting, non-possessive response which serves to set others free. Until this reality dawns upon them, the 'Six' person is all too easily swept up in all manner of fleeting (and often destructive) emotional encounters, particularly during their formative years.

It is only when they reach an understanding that all life forms are energised by a fragment of the Divine Creative Energy and respond by loving this portion of their Greater Self - without expectation of return - that a measure of that which is termed *Christ Consciousness* begins to develop within them. In so doing they reflect the higher vibration of the planet Venus which governs this number.

In their everyday life, the 'Six' person may well attract many who are lost and confused, drawn to them by the loving energy they project. In turn, they may - unthinkingly - begin to shoulder all manner of responsibility thrust upon them by these lost souls. Such actions are not always selfless, for those subject to this vibration have a deep need to be loved, but should such situations become onerous, they will quickly extricate themselves, moving on to something which is less threatening.

A great many opportunities wherein the 'Six' individual may demonstrate unconditional love will occur on the home front, wherein their great loyalty may be readily demonstrated. However, desperate to be loved, some among them could find themselves reduced to servitude within the home, a situation which eventually leads to bitter resentment. This should be avoided at all costs. They should also be on the alert for the destructive traits which this vibration can trigger, anxiety, habitual worrying and an argumentative nature.

Similarly, these people have a tendency to restrict their friends or associates to a small group, in whose life they will interfere, giving a great deal of gratuitous advice. 'Six' people should endeavour to 'add a friend a day' to their circle of associates and, in day- to-day encounters, smile at those who are obviously dejected or downcast. In this manner they not only uplift strangers, but also demonstrate the power of unconditional love.

Those seeking to master this vibration will be drawn to the Master Kuthumi for many different reasons, possibly because of the part He has played in their earlier life experiences, either as Pythagorus or as St. Francis of Assisi, or simply because they desire to play a conscious part in the Cosmic Scenario currently unfolding upon the planet - one which will see Kuthumi emerge as the World Teacher for the Aquarian Age. To this end they will need to stimulate the activation of their own Heart Chakra, and, through the power of unconditional love, encourage others to emulate them.

Seven

Governing those born on the 7th: 16th: & 25th:

'Seven' individuals tend to be extremely sensitive by nature and are easily bruised when subjected to the will - and unthinking actions - of others. This all too often results in a craving for the solitude of woodland and the harmonious world of nature. Introspective individuals, they are often fairly religious or spiritual in outlook and at some point in their life, may be called upon to make some form of sacrifice in order to fulfil their personal destiny.

Many among their number are extremely mediumistic and should learn to heed the still, inner voice which will provide them with the answers to many of the problems life holds for them. Some 'Seven' individuals find great personal satisfaction in the creative world of music and art, the inspiration they receive being channelled into a constructive undertaking, whilst others locate their sense of purpose via the focus of their mental faculties into the practical sciences.

As the planet Neptune governs this vibration, many who are subject to it may be inclined to gather possessions, which in time will possess them, all future action being coloured by the necessity to protect these. This, of course, is a blind alley from which they will have to emerge at some future point in time if they seriously desire to grow. For the majority, this may prove to be an extremely difficult lesson to learn, particularly as our materialistic society places great store on illusionary possessions.

Despondency and emotional imbalance have to be avoided,

as do illusions of all kinds, for they reflect the lower aspect of this vibration. 'Seven' individuals can be moody, melancholic and deeply critical, making them rather difficult companions.

With their energies positively channelled they can become fine examples of the power of spirit over matter, their intuitive powers providing hope and positive direction for those who would otherwise blunder through life. Success will be assured if they can but develop their capacity for self analysis, for this will lead them to a greater understanding of their purpose in life.

The Master Rakoczy will inspire those who endeavour to reflect the higher aspect of this vibration, particularly those who follow the occult or practical sciences, or those who are musically inclined. He is also concerned with mental out- growth particularly in Australia and North America.

Eight

Governing those born on the 8th: 17th: & 26th:

Endless difficulties appear to beset 'Eight' persons, the lives filled with petty restrictions and obstacles, all of which they have to learn to accept. As the result, a sad or gloomy outlook often characterises those who, as yet, cannot discern the purpose for this continual restriction.

The influence of the planet Saturn which governs this vibration serves to restrain our desires and activities, none of which is ever welcome. Yet, just as children have to learn to accept the disciplines of the adults who surround them (even though they may not understand the reasons), so the 'Eight' individual has to learn to accept that which is patently inevitable.

Those who incarnate to experience this particular life lesson tend to place great emphasis on material wealth and all that it can purchase, usually demanding the best in every category. To this end they are usually hardworking, becoming extremely practical and astute in business matters, or seeking to reach executive status within the world's major corporations, for they desire to be in control at all times. However, pride, impatience, intolerance and ruthlessness reflect the negative aspect of this vibration.

The major lesson which the Eight vibration has to teach lies in the development of awareness of the futility of material acquisition, perceiving this to be the great illusion that it is, one which masks a greater reality. The majority however will overlook this in their headlong rush for wealth and power. In the long term, Saturn the Initiator brings great rewards to those who learn his lessons well, and continued restaint to those who will not.

Some among them also seek to follow the Inner Way and to become the Initiate (the disciplined being) once more - a challenge they formerly faced in the mystery schools of earlier civilisations. As these no longer exist, the disciplines will be exacted of them in the outer world of matter, where they have little or no awareness of the reason for the many tests.

The Lord Maitreya, who is the Overseer for our planet and solar system endeavours to inspire those who are subject to this vibration to raise their level of consciousness and to play a part in His World Task, which involves the cleansing of the Etheric Body of the planet. Humanity pollutes this outer body of the earth with its negative thought patterns and the 'Eight' person, more than most, with their tendency to be angry, bitter or resentful in the face of undue restraint. His disciples should daily project a thought pattern of 'Light' toward and around the planet in a bid to speed up the necessary cleansing assisting, thereby the dawning of the New Age.

Nine

Governing those born on the 9th: 18th: & 27th:

This vibration is one which stimulates the desire to devote time and energy to caring for those in need and many born to experience it are to be found in the world's voluntary organisations, or channelling their energies into *Selfless Service* within the fields of medicine, scientific research or religion.

All 'Nine' individuals need to develop the sympathetic aspect of their natures seeking to acquire a bipartisan attitude toward human frailites. In volunteering to assist others in their hour of need, they should not look for or expect pecuniary reward, for so very often the greatest reward comes in the form of gratitude from those they endeavour to assist.

Such activities will in turn aid them to master one of life's great challenges, for it is only through loving and selfless service to others that they may expand their spiritual horizons. Where they do elect to serve mankind the 'Nine' person may well activate spiritual qualities or talents which are the fruits of their labours in earlier life experiences. Above all, the number nine identifies a lifetime wherein the individual concerned must endeavour to complete a task or undertaking commenced at another point in time.

As this vibration is governed by the planet Mars, those subject to it should try to curb their over - exhuberance and heed their bodily needs, for many among them can easily over-extend themselves in a surfeit of good works. This may then lead to serious health problems.

The negative side of this vibration is reflected in those who selfishly refuse to assist others - apart from close family members. All too often they become deeply embroiled in emotional relationships and may be predisposed toward dissipation or immorality.

The higher aspect of the nine vibration corresponds with that of the Master Jesus who will further stimulate the desire to serve others, for the greater joy it brings about. Equally, those gifted with the healing touch will become aware of His influence guiding them as they endeavour to aid those who are sick in mind, body or spirit.

Eleven

Governing those born on the 11th: & 29th:

Among those born to experience this particular vibration will be some who may well consider their life path to be greatly enriched by the influence of the planet Pluto. Others however may consider it to be nothing short of a curse, for Pluto is the planet of hidden karma, introducing many unexpected and unwelcome situations into their lives. Part of Pluto's task lies in bringing to the surface that which lies hidden and many of the situations these individuals will have to face relate to the skeletons they have hidden in the cupboard.

Being highly intuitive, the 'Eleven' person is at times subject to a deal of inspired thought, much of which fires their idealistic zeal. Rarely stopping to clarify the communication or to enquire how this might be applied in a practical manner, they rush off fully enthused in a bid to save the world.

Lacking a practical approach, their ideals are swiftly rejected and they retreat - often to cloud nine - to nurse their wounds. They then fire 'thunder bolts' of angry thought toward those who dared to disagree; a practice which is bound to intensify their sense of isoloation and - in the long term - to bring painful health conditions such as rheumatoid arthritis, in its wake. In extreme cases, insanity can result.

Those responding to the negative aspect of this vibration are invariably aimless, all too easily diverted into fanatical sects or beliefs. Once they have made a decision on a particular matter, they rarely wish to change their opinion, even though it is evident that the earlier decision was unwise. This rigid attitude will also cause health problems if it is maintained long term, leading to rigidity within the body.

As they tend to be somewhat trusting by nature it is important that the 'Eleven' individual learns to check the veracity of the statements made by others before acting upon them. Indeed, with regard to vitally important matters it would be as well to ensure that all agreements are legally binding.

The number eleven is one of two *over-vibrations* - its influence upon those who are subject to it being altogether different from that of the number two. Some schools of thought suggest the eleven be reduced to a two when undertaking a numerological chart, but in so doing, one overlooks the particular lessons attached to the number eleven. *Never* reduce eleven or add it to any other number. The numerologist should always highlight it and the difficult lessons associated with it.

The Lady Nada, whose vibration corresponds with the higher aspect of the number eleven, endeavours to stimulate New Age thinking in her disciples. This She achieves via the use of the Amethyst Ray - which is the healing ray for Aquarius. In addition She will seek to increase awareness of the healing forces and participation in one or more of the many healing techniques which are currently being reactivated world-wide.

This Illumined One appears on the Seventh Ray of Ritual and Ceremony which is currently influencing the thinking processes of humanity. Those who aspire to be her disciple will need to develop practicality of approach toward all idealistic concepts for life.

Twenty Two

This vibration is intended to produce the *Disciplined Soul* and is one of the most difficult on which to succeed, particularly for those of the feminine gender, who are often subject to the will of partners and family. This vibration will test their ability to remain calm and poised in all stressful situations. The majority find the 22 vibration to be an overwhelming experience, and often have difficulty in making descisions, so many among them spend much of their life sitting on the proverbial fence.

Vesta (a planetary force) governs this vibration and serves to rekindle awareness of our One - ness with the Creator. Those who are born on the twenty-second incarnate in an endeavour to demonstrate this truth in their humanitarian undertakings. Most among their number are down to earth, practical idealists whose aspiration is often international in its outlook, striving as they do toward world betterment.

Those who experience this vibration are subject to a deal of mental and emotional stress, which can result in a loss of ideals and in their developing an unbalanced outlook on life. In turn, this may well lead to a sense of inferiority. Success also eludes many among their number largely because they fail to exploit their latent talents. They may then elect to follow the negative aspect of this vibration, becoming indifferent to the needs of others and indulging in reckless or impractical activities.

These individuals would benefit greatly from the daily practice of introspection, focussing at days end, upon the events of the day. It is far better to undertake this in bed,first relaxing the body and then reviewing all activity - thoughts and actions - commencing at the end of the day and slowly searching backward to the start of the day. Where they discover a point in their day where their thoughts or actions were negative or destructive, they should endeavour to make amends by projecting a thought of *'Light'* coupled with one of *'Unconditional Love'* toward those they have wronged. This will provide a valuable insight into weaknesses of the personality enabling them to commence each day anew.

The second of the *'over vibrations'* , the number Twenty Two assumes great importance when undertaking a numerology chart and takes precedence over all other numbers. It should *never* be reduced to four or added to other numbers when seeking to locate the *Destiny Factor* or the *Overall Self Expression* lesson. Where twenty two does appear in a chart it should always be shown as the prime vibration governing the lesson concerned. (See example on page 144)

The Master Djwal Khul who, as a Second Ray Master is currently much involved with the instruction of many would-be disciples of other members of the Masters' Lodge, inspires those who endeavour to reflect the higher aspect of this vibration. Those who aspire to improve the quality of life via research in the world's laboratories or who serve in one of the many healing undertakings, receive the benefit of His stimulating energies, as do those who labour in welfare services world wide or in philanthropic movements such as the Red Cross.

Danger Signals

Apart from the numbers one to nine and the two *over-vibrations'* of eleven and twenty two, there are other vibrations which the numerologist should be alert to, for they do have a definite influence on the lives of those subject to them, yet often go unnoticed. They are those to which I apply the term *'Danger Signals'* . These are the numbers 13: 14: 16: and 19, all of which do eventually reduce to a single digit when undertaking a numerology chart - the number 13 reducing to 4 and so on. But there is a great need to forewarn those concerned of the difficulties which lie in wait along the path of life, difficulties which are highlighted by these Danger Signals. There are many schools of thought based upon the science of Numerology - many of which instruct the student to add all of the numbers located in a date of birth or name together, in order to reach a grand total. However, in so doing they overlook these extremely important lessons, awareness of which can make a vast amount of difference to how the individual concerned will respond to their life's lessons.

Thirteen

No number or colour can truly be said to be unlucky for luck, as it is termed, is something we create for ourselves. That which we term 'bad luck' is invariably born out of our responses (or the lack of them) to the situations we encounter in daily life.

The 'Thirteen' individual has the combined forces of the Sun, Jupiter and Uranus to contend with and as the result, would be well advised to keep their minds firmly focussed on the task in hand at all times.

Those born on the thirteenth tend to to allow their mind to wander from the task in hand, to a more stimulating situation which lies ahead of them. This all too often results in their overlooking minor, yet important details related to the task they currently undertake. The effects of their inattention to detail will be revealed at a later point in time when everything collapses around them.

Furthermore, they often experience a measure of difficulty in completing an undertaking, their enthusiam being fired by far more tempting activities, causing them to leave their original task incomplete. They may further compound the situation by abandoning the second task in order to attend to something left incomplete the previous day . This results in a number of incomplete tasks and great confusion. The major lesson which this particular Danger Signal has to teach is the necessity to keep one's mind firmly affixed on the task in hand and to complete one undertaking at a time.

Thirteen does reduce to four and therefore those subject to it will be possessed of a strong will and a rigid outlook on life. The lower aspect of this vibration is also reflected in an inability to focus the mind on any subject for any length of time.

Fourteen

The energies of the planet Mercury are well to the fore within his vibration, in addition to those of the Sun and Uranus under which the 'Fourteen' individuals must learn to control their quicksilver thought and speech. The Danger Signal here forewarns of the tendency to criticise the actions of others. Where such criticism is not of a constructive nature these individuals would be well advised to hold their tongues unless they wish to pay the price in some form of 'instant karma'.

Those subject to this particular vibration should also bear in mind the fact that where their sweeping criticism eventuates in a cessation of growth in those they have so readily criticised, then they must be prepared to bear a portion of the karma of failure which will then eventuate.

The Elder Brothers teach that the habit of criticising others reveals a fatal flaw in the character of those who indulge in it, whilst serving to draw attention to the fact that they have not yet learned to control their emotional nature. Rather than resorting to criticism, the 'Fourteen' individuals should try to illustrate a positive course of action which the persons under review may then attempt to follow.

Criticism rarely changes anyone. Indeed it may have quite the opposite effect, and may well serve to intensify a dogged determination to reject unsought advice, no matter how well intentioned. With their critical faculties

firmly   under control and their mental powers put to
positive use, those born on this day may well emerge as
constructive forces within the community, teaching others by
their own positive examples.

Sixteen

The life pattern of those born on this day can be somewhat difficult, for although they are quite psychic they rarely put their perceptivity to work in matters appertaining to the self. All too trusting by nature they are easily mislead by the illusionary suggestions made by others and suffer as the result. All 'Sixteen' people should learn to check and double check every situation or opportunity before committing themselves to action of any kind.

The Sun, Venus and Neptune will influence the outcome of this life providing the potential for positive leadership in the field of spiritual awareness - always provided that all service is undertaken in the spirit of unconditional love. Due to their extreme sensitivity, the majority of those born on this day need a peaceful and relaxing environment and when under stress should seek temporary refuge within the realm of nature. However, their labours lie within the cities where the lost and the confused await them.

With regard to their undoubted mediumistic capacities they should *at all times* strive to raise their level of consciousness to communicate with the Teachers of the Higher Sub-plane of the Mental Plane, determinedly rejecting the illusionary communications which emanate from the Astral Realm. To this end they should insist on proof of the validity of any communication received, particularly those which appertain to themselves.

Nineteen

This vibration can prove to be one of the most difficult to master, for in addition to the illusions of the Plane of Matter these individuals will also need to become master of the self. Very early in life they should come to the realisation that they will only obtain from life what they are personally prepared to put into it.

The Sun and the planet Mars influence this vibration and together will encourage those born on this day to seek self expression in those undertakings wherein they might serve others. Any inclination to dominate or drive others against their will in a bid to achieve a personal goal must, at all costs, be avoided. The true achievers on this vibration are those who, by their personal example, demonstrate positive leadership.

Due to their natural capacity for leadership and their ambitious natures, the 'Nineteen' individuals could easily reach the executive level within the world's major business corporations, where the sheer brilliance of their creative and imaginative abilities would capture the attention of others.

Failure occurs on this vibration when the individual concerned decides to 'opt out' of society, declining to serve others, preferring to focus their attention upon fulfilling their own personal desires. This will eventuate in an empty, aimless existence, the outcome of which may be a deep resentment directed toward those whose lives appear to be full and satisfying. Such negativity will almost certainly result in painful health disorders further down the track.

Those subject to this vibration should take care not to become self-centred, endeavouring wherever possible to see anothers point of view. Any tendency to repress the emotions must also be guarded against, this negative trait being replaced by a frank and open manner if they wish to avoid ill-health.

The Personality Factor

The inital phase of the life behind them, each individual now embarks upon a phase of expression wherein the personality comes to the fore. This usually commences around the age of twenty-eight, but for some individuals this can commence around the age of twenty-five.   The personality itself is the mask of the soul and during the first twenty-eight years is subject to the influence of the *Governing Factor* vibration, but during the middle phase of the life it emerges to express itself as a definite entity.

This cycle will also take twenty-eight years to complete and its lesson is located within the numeric pattern associated with the month of birth.   Nonetheless, the personality will still subject to the influence of the Governing Factor vibration, which is the primary lesson for the overall lifetime.

To ascertain the lesson which the personality must now learn, the month of the birth must be given a numerical equivalent, but there is also a need to study the date of birth to ascertain if there are any hidden Danger Signals which the personality should be alerted to. For instance where someone was born on the 12th of June 1963, the date of birth should be reduced as follows:

12th   June   1963
3   +   6   +   19 -1   Total = 1

Here we find a Danger Signal located within the year of

the birth and the person concerned would have to be fore-warned of this when undertaking a chart on their behalf. (Refer to page 72 for an explanation of how I have arrived at these totals.)

The Personality Factor lesson for this individual amounts to Six and until they reach the age of fifty-six they will have to strive to master this lesson, which appertains to the sharing of love in a totally unconditional manner with all whom they encounter in daily life - a somewhat daunting task!

However had our subject been born on the 12th of November 1963 great caution would have to be exercised in its translation if we are not to overlook a vital pointer for the person concerned.

$$12th \quad November \quad 1963$$
$$3 \quad + \quad 11 \quad + \quad 19 = 1 \quad = 11 + 4$$

The pitfall for the unwary lies within the Over-Vibration of 11, which must **never** be reduced to a single digit, but used to serve as an indicator of how the Destiny Factor (the sum total of the birth date) might be arrived at. In this example the Destiny Factor is in fact 11 plus 4 - idealism to be expressed through a practical and down-to-earth approach.

Were the 11 of the Personality Factor lesson to be reduced to 2 (as some schools of thought teach) and then added to the remainder of the birth date to arrive at the Destiny Factor lesson, this would amount to 6, indicating a need to learn to express unconditional love for all mankind. Yet their true lesson lies in expressing their high ideals (11) in a constructive and practical manner (4) - an entirely different outlook upon life!

Time now to study the various Personality Factor lessons, bearing in mind that each is undertaken in conjunction with the more powerful influence of the Governing Factor in view, then put this knowledge to work on the following Work Space page.

Work Space

Date of Birth:

Reducing to:

Governing Factor:

Personality Factor:

Conclusion:

Date of Birth:

Reducing to:

Governing Factor:

Personality Factor:

Conclusion:

One

Influencing those born in January and October

With this vibration the ego has the opportunity to prove to all and sundry its ability to stand alone, quite independent of others and that, despite thoughts to the contrary, they do have a capacity to lead.

The positive influence of the Sun will stimulate all thought and action, providing the strength and motivation for whatever these individuals seek to undertake. Those who are born in October may achieve much more than those born in January, for the added influence of the naught will further strengthen their determination to become totally independent.

Opportunities which will assist them in the conscious development of all masculine traits will come their way, largely due to the influence of the Sun, but success will depend entirely upon the self-image these individuals project. With determination and courage even the greatest of obstacles can be overcome.

In seeking to demonstrate the power of their newly developed personality the 'One' individual must endeavour not to tread rough-shod over others, but to demonstrate their leadership capacity by example alone. In this manner they will gain willing cooperation. On the reverse side of this vibration we find those who fail this lesson in a big way. They may act like shrinking, nocturnal blossoms, retreating from any form of public activity, rejecting all proffered opportunities for responsibility, clinging instead to others for support.

Two

Influencing those born in February

The lessons which 'Two' personalities have to master are quite the reverse of those of the 'One' individual. Influenced by the Moon they do not have what it takes to become great world leaders, nor are they likely to be happy living alone. Therefore they must learn to adapt to the stronger wills of those who surround them if they are to enjoy any measure of happiness. Great joy can be found by sharing the great fount of love and affection they have locked within the self.

Any tendency to play King Canute - refusing to acknowledge the power of the tide of opinion which is against them - is almost certain to result in a deal of emotional conflict and turmoil. During this phase of the lifetime 'Two's' have to learn to accept that others have the upper hand and adjust their thinking accordingly. Cultivation of the art of diplomacy would prove to be a great asset.

This will certainly be an extremely emotional phase of life with the tendency to react in an overly sensitive manner to the words and actions of others. This is due to the influence of the Moon which may also cause these individuals to sink into the depths of despair.

In bid to rise above the emotional tide, 'Two's' should endeavour to express their innate sensitivity by developing artistic or creative qualities, particularly if these can be expressed within the home environment.

Those who refuse to unbend or to make any attempt to adapt to the will of others, sinking instead into dark despair, will almost certainly fail this lesson, as will those who seek peace at any price, for these traits mark a weakness of character guaranteed to ensure a return match at some future point in time.

Three

Influencing those born in March and December

This is one of the more enjoyable vibrations for the personality to experience, for this segment of the life will be filled with many pleasurable encounters or situations, as the planet Jupiter governs this vibration.

As self expression is the watchword here, the best possible advice which could be offered to 'Three' personalities is "go out and prove to all and sundry just how talented you really are". With encouragement from the Venetian Master, the field of the arts will be open to them and the world will be their oyster, no matter in which direction their talents lie, be it creative art-work, colour, fashion, music or the world of communications.

Those 'Three' personalities who prefer the quiet backwaters of married life will locate countless opportunities to demonstrate their many skills - in the culinary arts, the creation of a bright and colourful environment or in fashioning a restful garden.

Social life will be highlighted with this vibration with 'Three' individuals becoming very popular on the social scene. They should however take care not to neglect their many talents even though emphasis will be placed on the development of the personality.

Some 'Three' personalities, lacking in the social graces, will feel inadequate and be unwilling to participate in social gatherings and, where pressured to attend, will retreat to a far corner feeling miserable and ignored. They must bear in mind that we become that which we think, and if they look upon themselves as chameleons who change colour to blend in with their environment, they can hardly complain when their subterfuge succeeds!

Four

Influencing those born in April

There are two options open to 'Four' personalities, either to work hard and become pillars of society or to abuse their will power and become the local guerilla leader.

Uranus, the planet of the will governs this vibration and the lower aspect brings in its wake strong-willed reactions and rebellious tendencies, whilst on the positive front these individuals can demonstrate the highly practical side of their nature, accepting limitations and building for a positive future.

The majority of 'Four' individuals are inclined to be hardworking and industrious, shunning the glitter of the social world, considering it to be transitory and without value. They need to take care that such an outlook does not eventually dominate to the point where all forms of pleasurable activity are shunned in favour of work. To do so is to earn the title of 'kill-joy' among their associates. In all life there must be balance and simple joys and pleasures taken as respite from industrious effort are not necessarily wrong.

Where these individuals determinedly utilise their will-power in a destructive manner, resisting any form of change which does not correspond with their personal desires, or in rebelling against law and order, they will bring retribution upon their heads and fail with this particular lesson. But, with the will firmly under control and utilised in a constructive manner, 'Four' individuals can emerge as a powerful force within the community.

Five

Influencing those born in May

The frivolous side of the nature will surface under this vibration and as 'Five' personalities do not welcome restriction of any kind, particularly with regard to their thought patterns, emotional responses or actions , they could well end up as Jacks (or Jills) - of-all-Trades unless they heed the lessons this vibration has to teach.

With their general distate for responsibility, the majority of those who must experience this vibration will find the attention of the Master Serapis somewhat uncomfortable to say the least, emphasising as He does the necessity to focus all thought and action upon undertakings which will benefit mankind.

A career as a commercial salesperson would suit them admirably, providing all of the freedom they desire - constant change and travel, coupled with unlimited opportunities to put their silver tongues to good use.

Gifted though they are, many 'Five' individuals will seek to avoid the responsibility which would eventuate were they to successfully develop their natural talents. Yet if they are to achieve any measure of growth during this period,they will need to grasp every opportunity that influential people will offer them.

The lower aspect of the Five vibration encourages involvement in illusionary practices and many of those subject to it will be greatly fascinated by one or more of these, with promiscuous behaviour, alchohol and narcotics being particularly attractive. All 'Five' personalities need to exercise great caution in this direction for any of these indulgences could easily overwhelm them, resulting in abject failure and possible negative karma.

Six

Influencing those born in June

The majority of those subject to this vibration will have an overwhelming need to be loved but will soon learn that this has to be earned. It is only when they begin to love others - *without expectation of return* - that the love they crave will flow toward them.

The negative aspect of this vibration is marked by possessiveness and jealousy, traits which will soon cause love to wither upon the vine. The 'Six' person needs to devote a deal of time to cultivating friendships, expanding their circle of friends wherever possible and should endeavour to overcome the tendency to meddle in the lives of others.

The lower aspect of the six vibration also encourages a superficial quality, particularly in relationships, with the 'Six' person skilfully ending these once they become irksome. However, if they are to avoid lonliness in later life they should endeavour to be constant and supportive of others in their hour of need. Relationships do bring a measure of responsibility and the 'Six' person must be prepared to accept this.

The path which the 'Six' person treads under this vibration may prove to be difficult at times , but if they can learn to set aside all thought of self and come to love others for the simple joy this brings about, then they are well on the way toward achieving their goal.

Seven

Influencing those born in July

A vibration that brings great sensitivity, one which may prove difficult to master. Indeed, it is only by learning to heed the 'still inner voice' that the 'Seven' personalities can hope to achieve success. Easily hurt by the responses of those they encounter in daily life, many among them begin to feel that they are 'the odd one out' amongst their circle of associates. As the result many of these individuals become reclusive.

They may also find the pressures of city life overwhelming and long for the solace of the world of nature. Despite this, their role as an intermediary between the 'seen and the unseen' means that they have to dwell amidst those who are lost and confused, much to their dis-satisfaction.

Many 'Seven' individuals refuse to acknowledge the mediumistic aspect of their nature, electing to develop their mental faculties instead which they then channel into the practical sciences.

However the influence of the planet Neptune which governs this vibration brings the mediumistic ability to the fore and this may lead to a deal of mental and emotional confusion. These individuals must be aware - at all times - of the negative aspect of this vibration, namely illusion, fear and over-sensitivity - to which they may easily fall prey!

Eight

Influencing those born in August

"Oh death, where is thy sting?' could well be the plaintive cry of those who must experience this rather difficult vibration, for death could well be the only trauma missing from their lives. Deep within the self lies the strength and the courage to overcome the never-ending tests to which they will be subject, for none is ever permitted to undertake tasks which are beyond their capacity to endure.

In the past all would-be initiates undertook their training within the Mystery Schools and had therefore, some awareness of what lay ahead of them. Such schools alas, no longer exist and the aspiring initiate must now undergo their training in the outer world surrounded by all manner of temptation. They must swiftly learn that the true initiate overcomes the seemingly impossible by ceasing to resist and willingly accepting the necessity for that which is patently inevitable - and to do so with a smile!

Saturn, the Relentless Reaper (also known as the Great Initiator) governs this phase of the lifetime and apart from the necessary cleansing situations all must undergo at his command, the Eight Personalities will discover that he also brings monetary energies to the fore and these will also require firm handling. The business world will beckon during this central phase of the life and some 'Eight's' could well emerge as stars of the commercial world - provided that they are willing to put their shoulders to the wheel and prove to others just what may be achieved through sheer hard work and dogged determination.

Failure will eventuate if they reject or resent opposition and refuse to accept the situations which are presented to them. Such responses can lead to bitterness and a life of ill-health, arising solely from their long-term resentful thought patterns.

Nine

Influencing those born in September

During this segment of their lives, the 'Nine' Personalities must ponder on just how to put their caring nature to the best possible use without depleting their energy levels in the process. Strong Martian energies will provide the drive to accomplish many selfless tasks, particularly the undertaking of good works in the community. This selfless outlook will be further stimulated by the energies of the Master Jesus who endeavours to inspire those who seek to master this particular vibration.

In electing to experience the 'Nine' vibration these individuals are endeavouring to complete a task commenced during an earlier life experience and no matter what task or undertaking they initiate during this central phase of the lifetime, it must be taken to its point of conclusion. They should not therefore set in motion any task which cannot be brought to fruition before the end of this current cycle (by the age of fifty-six).

Those 'Nine' personalities who, like Nero before them, 'fiddle whilst Rome burns' are, in ignoring the cries for help around and about them, reflecting the negative characteristics which this vibration stimulates. In selfishly satisfying their own whims and desires and ignoring the needs of others - refusing to play the Good Samaritan as they should - they are headed for failure and should not be surprised when others avoid them or refuse to assist in their own hour of need.

Eleven

Influencing those born in November.

Although they may well be inclined to take up hot-air ballooning, the 'Eleven' Personalities would be well advised to buy a pair of deep-sea divers boots instead for they are all too prone to float off on 'cloud nine' forgetful of reality. There is a great necessity for these individuals to come down to terra firma and to endeavour to remain earthed.

They are possessed at times of the most inventive and idealistic concepts for life, all of which could possibly be of enormous benefit to humanity. However, their solutions lack practicality and their ideals tend to be rejected by others. If they are to succeed in putting their ideas for world betterment into action, they need to develop a realistic and practical approach to all such undertakings.

Possessed of highly intuitive natures the 'Eleven' Personalities should endeavour to develop this quality, seeking inspiration from the Teachers on the higher sub-plane of the Mental Plane, acquiring thereon a practical solution for world problems.

The planet Pluto which governs this vibration brings all that which is hidden to the surface. Therefore these individuals should prepare for a number of unpleasant surprises during this central phase of the lifetime, with all manner of skeletons being dragged from their hiding place, for Pluto is the Planet of Hidden Karma.

Constantly refusing to alter their opinions in the face of opposition, together with frequent withdrawal to cloud nine can lead to serious health problems, particularly osteo-arthritis and insanity.

The Maturity Factor

This lesson is located within the sum total of the **Year of Birth** and, as with all other numbers, should be reduced wherever possible to a single digit, the exceptions being the Over Vibrations of 11 and 22.

For instance, where the year of birth was 1924 the numerologist should add this together in a bid to reach an overall total. Add the 1 to 9 making ten, plus the 2 making twelve and finally the 4 to arrive at a total of 16.   This must of course be reduced to 7 in the final analysis, but do bear in mind the fact that 16 is a Danger Signal of which the person concerned must be forewarned.

During this final phase of experience the individual, matured by time and experience seeks to complete all of its pre-selected goals, mastering during this final phase the numerical vibration which governs it. Commencing between the   fiftieth and fifty-sixth year   this   vibration   will provide   the opportunity   for   positive   expression based   upon   the knowledge acquired during earlier cycles.

Once   again,   heed   the   dominating   influence of the Governing Factor   lesson which still influences all thought and action, indicating just how the individual will respond to the influence of this further vibration. By the time the individual reaches this period in   their   life-cycle they should be well aware of their Destiny Factor vibration, taking steps to ensure success in that direction also.

As the physical energies begin to wane, mental activity and soul searching take over as we seek to discover the specific purpose for life. Following the complex - and often contradictory - vibrations can lead to all manner of difficulties, but with determination we can all pull off the unexpected.

Before moving on to study the various lessons attached to the Maturity Factor there are some valid points to note. Take the following date of birth.

12th	November	1966
3	11	22

It is *not* possible to overlook the fact that two of these numbers are *Over-Vibrations* and simply reduce these to facilitate translation. These vibrations indicate an individual of extreme sensitivity with enormous potential for humanitarian endeavours. To reduce the 11 to 2 and the 22 to 4 would be to completely overlook the inner intent of this person. Each phase of their life would need to be viewed in conjunction with his or her idealistic tendencies, with firm warnings on the necessity for practicality at all times. Take great care to emphasise the lessons so indicated, for we are entering a difficult period of experience on the Planet Earth and require great practicality from our visionaries.

In a situation such as that shown in this example the numerologist would need to place emphasis upon the strongest vibration - that of the number 22 - and use this as a denominator ie: the Maturity Factor lesson would be thus:

$$22 + 11 + 3$$

Here the humanitarian aspect of the nature is to be expressed within an undertaking where their responsible nature and leadership qualities (22), together with a practical approach to idealism (11) can lead to a deal of self expression (3). In such undertakings great care should be taken to avoid the tendency to be indecisive, refusing to develop latent talent, or retreating in the face of opposition.

Work Space

Date of Birth:

Reducing to:

Governing Factor:

Personality Factor:

Maturity Factor:

Conclusion:

Date of Birth:

Reducing to:

Governing Factor:

Personality Factor:

Maturity Factor:

Conclusion:

One

Time to gaze back upon those situations commenced with a flourish amid earlier bursts of enthusiasm but which, for one reason or another, simply did not work out as planned. With a more mature outlook these individuals may now pick up the pieces and apply a new approach or fresh originality to them, bringing the embers back to life.

Quite often this is a period wherein 'One' individuals become aware of their true selves, where they often have to stand alone, fate having taken a hand in shaping their destinies. Time now to prove to those who watch anxiously from the sidelines that they are more than capable of 'doing their own thing' without the support of others.

Provided that they have retained their individuality throughout life and maintained activities which stimulate mentally and physically, this can prove to be a very positive cycle of experience, one which will be largely devoid of the emotional conflicts that may have marred the earlier cycles.

During this closing phase of the life experience the stimulating energies of the Master Hilarion may prove to be extremely beneficial, encouraging all manner of independant thought and action.

Two

The home-front may well have been the major point of focus during this lifetime and it may now appear to be cold and empty. Those upon whom Two's have showered love and affection (and who in turn gave life a sense of purpose) have now withdrawn to create lives of their own. Time therefore to take stock, to look for new fields of endeavour wherein they may now demonstrate their diplomatic skills in addition to their uncanny abilities to draw loose ends together to make a perfect whole.

The Lady Mary brings her influence to bear at this point in their lives encouraging these individuals to look within for inspiration and direction, which may in turn be shared with others who have similar needs.

During this final cycle of experience many subject to this lesson look towards community projects or to one of the many voluntary organisations which offer challenging outlets for the talents they have so patiently nurtured throughout life. The 'Two' individuals may locate a sense of satisfaction in service undertaken within those organisations which require a deal of loving patience and personal experience, such as marriage guidance, the Samaritans or one of the Lifeline projects.

Time and experience should have taught them the necessity for detachment in emotional situations and provided that they maintain this, they can offer invaluable assistance and support to those caught up in emotional storms and entanglements.

Three

During this cycle, many who are subject to this lesson come into full bloom, all restrictions having melted away, whether self-imposed or otherwise. They should now find great delight in expressing their latent abilities for many opportunities will now be offered to them. Their artistic talents can certainly be developed and expressed with great panache, largely due to the guiding influence of the Venetian Master. Self expression through colour, sound or form will bring great personal satisfaction during this final phase of the lifetime.

This will also be a period in which social activities may feature high on their list of priorities, for light-hearted discussion, dancing, theatre parties, even the local bridge or bowls club will offer many opportunities for light-hearted banter and warm companionship.

Due to a new-found charisma these individuals may also be drawn into joyous romantic attachments, all of them fleeting, for they greatly value their new-found freedom, particularly the many opportunities provided for self-expression. Vital growth can be achieved during this most stimulating of closing cycles.

Four

The influence of the Master El Morya combined with the powerful stimulation of the planet Uranus will bring the will-power to the fore during this final cycle of experience. All too often this will stimulate a grim determination to attain that which was denied during earlier phases of the life. Provided that they are practical in their approach to monetary matters during this final cycle - and practicality is the keyword - then fairly early in this period these individuals should be able to step aside, passing the reins of authority to others in order that they too may begin to assume a portion of responsibility.

However many who are born to experience this particular vibration 'die with their boots on', so attached do they become to workaday patterns. Those who are about to undergo the '4' vibration should be aware that it will stimulate a deal of activity in practical fields of endeavour. They should also be aware that intensive labour during this final segment of the lifetime may well shorten the life-span.

If these individuals can but bring themselves to let go of the reins of power they will find ample time to enjoy the remainder of their lives, exploring the inner-self and the world at large. Sadly many will find such pastimes and suggestions distasteful, for having got the bit between their teeth they are not inclined to let go. If they must work, then they should endeavour to do so without placing undue stress upon their physical form, delegating authority and becoming benign overseers . . . if that is at all possible.

Five

During this final cycle of experience, those of the male gender who are subject to the 'Five' vibration are often inclined to act out of character, throwing up steady careers and running off with their typist, or simply throwing caution to the winds and becoming involved in every conceivable situation from which they had withheld their energies during earlier cycles. They often embark on world travel, become involved in 'way-out' philosophies or the occult. If it is 'out there' at this point in their life, 'Five' individuals will seek to experience it.

Those of the feminine gender will not be far behind them as they will be determined not to be left by the wayside, for they are by no means ready for the quiet backwaters of life or the old folks home. Many become trendy, the latest fashion is there to be experienced, together with the latest hair design or colour, the more outrageous the better.

Discussion groups, amateur theatre, spiritualism, indeed any field where communication of some form may be experienced, will draw these individuals. Some among them may even blossom into best-selling authors, provided they can find the time to sit down and write! Such activity is the reflection of their response to the influence the Master Serapis exerts upon their minds. He it is who encourages the channelling of their creative faculties into positive undertakings, resulting in growth and expansion.

Six

This signals an interesting phase in life, bringing into being all that which the 'Six' individual has longed for but which was denied during earlier life cycles. Love will take on a new meaning in life where they will see, perhaps for the first time, the necessity to love for the sheer joy this brings about, careless of whether or not they are loved in return. Love of this nature invariably strikes a chord within others who sense the lack of strings or ties and respond accordingly.

Reactions such as this are a response to the influence of the Master Kuthumi and can, in turn, lead to meaningful relationships - devoid of the torrid passion which may have marked earlier experiences. Sincere companionship may then develop along with a measure of stability on monetary levels. During this closing cycle their skilful use of colour will come into prominence and they will have the opportunity to create dream homes or gardens of unsurpassed beauty, which could well be the envy of all.

Seven

'Seven' individuals will be presented with many opportunities for relaxation during this cycle of experience, possibly within the gentle vibrations of the countryside which they so love, finding there the peace their souls crave. Nonetheless this will be a period wherein they must seek to come to terms with the unknown, exploring its far horizons.

Once familiar with the higher realms of consciousness, they must then endeavour to assist those in need, particularly those who lack the 'Seven's' natural mediumistic skills. The guiding hand of the Master Rakoczy will be clearly evident within such undertakings, presenting ever greater challenges and opportunities for service.

This will eventually lead to great demands and pressures being placed upon those individuals who, having become extremely sensitive, may desire to withdraw from the hurly-burly of everyday life. However they need to adopt a simple outlook upon life, perceiving this as an overall experience and not merely a series of unrelated incidents. They should also endeavour to express all that which flows unbidden into their minds, born as it is, of a higher intelligence.

This intelligence seeks to assist humanity in its struggle to come to terms with the illusionary plane of matter and 'Seven' individuals have a vital role to play in that struggle. Above all this is a cycle wherein these persons must come to terms with their innate mediumistic capacities, seeing them for the blessings they are and not the curse others would have them believe.

Eight

For those embarking upon this final cycle of experience the planet Saturn will offer assistance on one of two fronts. His energies may either stimulate a desire for material success, reactivating those dreams or ambitions which failed to materialise during earlier character building cycles. Or the Saturnian influence may encourage them to seek out disciplines which will bring about inner illumination. Whichever course of action they elect to follow, the going will be challenging and arduous.

Being the disciplinarian all of mankind requires from time to time, Saturn can stimulate material growth, provided that 'Eight' individuals will learn to accept the restrictions which will be placed upon personal desires as a necessary part of a greater plan. In bending the knee and learning to accept the inevitable they could be on their way to monumental success becoming, perhaps, the guiding lights within the business fraternity. However if embarking upon this course of action they should be prepared to die in harness.

On the reverse side of the coin, conscious acceptance of continual restraint can result in the dawning of an inner awareness which is beyond price, coupled with a measure of spiritual attainment that nothing can surpass. If selecting this pathway, the influence of the Lord Maitreya will be an undoubted asset for He seeks to inspire and stimulate all who are prepared to sublimate the lower will and search for greater awareness.

Nine

Not only does this vibration mark the final cycle of the current life-span but it also signifies the completion of a much earlier cycle of experience, one commenced long, long ago. Here is the opportunity for 'Nine' individuals to prove that they have absorbed all the lessons of their long-gone past and acquired full realisation that the self is but a part of a greater whole.

Numerous opportunities for selfless service to their fellow men and women will present themselves, wherein they may demonstrate this philosophical outlook. Such service will carry within it the seeds of future growth. The inspiration of the Master Jesus - who guides the steps of those who seek to master this vibration - will provide a constant source of strength and support.

In endeavouring to follow this pathway, many upon it will be subject to intense pressure for a great many calls will be made upon their time and energy. They should however learn to be practical and conserve their physical energy. Where they continually deplete this it could result in damage to the physical form and prevent them from aiding others who wait in the wings. Like a complex machine the human form has many parts which are subject to wear and tear and these individuals may well have reached that point in life where certain organs no longer function as they once did.

Overall this is a cycle within which they may demonstrate unselfish thought and action. This of itself may bring its due return, for none labours within the Father/Mother's vineyard without just reward.

Eleven

Under the watchful eye of the Lady Nada individuals who are subject to this lesson commence a cycle of experience wherein that which lies dormant within the self can be expected to rise to the surface. They should be prepared to come face to face with that which they are, as the energy of the planet Pluto begins to affect their thoughts and actions. During this final phase, ideals will become a conscious point of focus, but unless these can be demonstrated in a practical manner they are doomed to rejection by humanity.

If past cycles have taught them the necessity for practicality this may well prove to be one of the most fruitful cycles of the current life-span, for the spiritually aware among us are ever seeking new methods to improve the quality of life and to expand self-awareness. Provided that 'Elevens' are able to illustrate positive and practical methods whereby either of these may be realised, those who are in search of enlightenment will beat loudly upon their doors.

Overall this will prove to be a very sensitive cycle of experience, during which they may receive 'communications from on high'. Caution is urged in this direction however, for few will understand this aspect of their nature. They should therefore refrain from boasting that they 'hear voices', unless they wish to be placed in safe institutions. The very fact that they have developed a 'sixth sense' is not necessarily welcomed in a three dimensional world.

Twenty Two

To ensure success upon this vibration these individuals will need to be in complete control of their thoughts and emotions, and should endeavour to analyse these at day's end to ensure that negativity does not become a permanent fixture in their lives. Here we locate the Disciplined Souls, incarnate to demonstrate One-ness with the Father/Mother God and needing to be perfectly balanced - on all levels - at all times. Conscious, daily attunement to the energy of the Master Djwal Khul could well provide the required measure of stimulus, for His energies direct the footsteps of all who struggle with this most difficult of lessons.

Vesta is the governing planetary influence here, stimulating awareness of the need to become permanent illustrations of the power of spirit over matter. As potential Disciplined Souls they have returned to demonstrate just what can be achieved by spiritually awakened beings .

Success is bound to follow their conscious efforts as others become involved in their idealistic and practical concepts for life and endeavour to bring about their fulfillment. The 'Twenty Two's' should always be mindful of the invaluable assistance others render in bringing their dreams to fruition and they should be prepared to acknowledge this publicly.

Failure occurs when they lose sight of their ideals, allowing petty restrictions and obstacles to create imbalance. It is extremely difficult to be successful upon this vibration - particularly for married women - who are so often subject to the whims of loved ones.

The Destiny Factor

This lesson relates to the total outcome of life and is secondary only to the energy of the Governing Factor vibration. Nonetheless it could be considered to be the most vital lesson which an individual seeks to master, for it provides the theme for the overall life experience, and is that which the Higher Self desires to master.

The energy of the *Destiny Factor* vibration will colour all thought and responses and could perhaps be likened to a shimmering mirage upon the far horizon. For many it will remain as such if they fall by the wayside, allowing the sensual nature, activated by a series of minor challenges encountered en route, to dominate thought and action.

To fail upon this lesson ensures a return match at some future point in time, in a bid to regain control of those aspects of the self which led to failure. The overall purpose for life in this world of matter is to attain perfection through repeated embodiments, experiencing all which this world has to teach us. We may reduce the necessity for continual incarnation if we can but grasp the purpose for this current lifetime.

Quite often the Destiny Factor brings forward lessons that may have been deliberately avoided during earlier life experiences and which may prove difficult to overcome. In such situations, the individuals concerned may have to battle with negativity for much of their lifetime, thus learning to bring their wayward thought patterns under control. As such points are more clearly understood when demonstrated, let us consider the following example.

Date of Birth:	16th April 1942
Reducing to:	7 4 (16) = 7 Total = 9 (Note here that the Danger Signal 16 appears twice. Issue strong warning against illusion of all kinds).
Governing Factor: = 7	(Danger Signal 16). Highly sensitive and mediumistic. Inclined toward illusionary pastimes.
Personality Factor: = 4	Practical approach toward life with an ability to organise others.
Maturity Factor: = 7	(Danger Signal 16)A doubly sensitive cycle. Avoid all illusionary situations or communications.
Destiny Factor: = 9	Completion of an earlier incarnation. Selfless service to mankind essential.

Conclusion: Here we have an individual whose allotted task involves the need to come to terms with his or her highly sensitive nature, whilst seeking to develop undoubted mediumistic abilities, taking care to bypass the illusionary astral planers which interpenetrate this world of matter.

This individual should also avoid involvement in transitory emotional encounters or illusionary pursuits. (With two 16's featuring so prominently in the life lessons, alchohol, narcotic substances and sensual activities could well prove to be irresistible). Furthermore, the 9 of the Destiny Factor will serve to enhanmce their desire to serve in the field of mediumistic endeavour.

Despite the foregoing, there may well be a powerful disinclination to undertake any form of service, for this individual appears to have rejected such opportunities during earlier life experiences (identified by the presence of the two '16' Danger Signals). However, if so motivated, they must ensure that such service is not undertaken simply for material gain. As both the Governing Factor and the Destiny Factor (the primary vibrations) respond to the number 16, there is an overwhelming necessity to master the illusions of this Plane of Matter during the current life experience.

During the secondary phase of this lifetime - which occurs between the 28th and 56th year, he or she faces the task of developing a highly practical and disciplined approach to life. However, as they are so very sensitive, this may prove to be a difficult undertaking and their response to a great many situations may well be resentment or rebellion against authority or law and order. Thus, only the constructive application of their willpower will enable them to achieve success during this particular phase in life.

Their pathway will be strewn with all manner of illusionary pitfalls during the final cycle of experience, for here the second Danger Signal 16 emerges to further influence thoughts and actions. This will serve to intensify the illusionary tendencies which the Governing Factor has so far encouraged. This individual may well have an ever increasing desire to flee from people and civilisation seeking tranquility in country surroundings, yet the vibrations they have incarnated to master indicate the necessity to remain among the masses and expand their mediumistic talents.

This person is likely to experience a great deal of nervous stress in coming to terms with a somewhat difficult life-pattern, responding in a highly emotional manner to most day-to-day situations. They will require patient counselling on how it is often their own negative responses to most situations which are the underlying cause of their problems.

With this example in mind study the various Destiny Factor lessons and put them into operation on the workspace provided.

Work space

Date of Birth:

Reducing to:

Governing Factor:

Personality Factor:

Maturity Factor:

Destiny Factor:

Conclusion:

Date of Birth:

Reducing to:

Governing Factor:

Personality Factor:

Maturity Factor:

Destiny Factor:

Conclusion:

One

This vibration carries the stimulating energy of the Sun which is enhanced by the powerful influence of the Master Hilarion. The path of destiny could possibly be described as that which fashions courageous leaders. For those whose destiny this is, success or failure will be entirely dependent on their ability to make decisions and to act swiftly upon them. Those among them who are given to indecision will not find this to be a particularly enjoyable lifetime.

'One' individuals must be prepared to stand or fall by that which they initiate, providing at all times positive and dynamic leadership, either within their home environment, the business world, local politics, or within one of the many voluntary organisations. In common with the valiant kings of old, 'One' individuals have to be seen to be playing their part to the full - at the very centre of any battle - providing a rallying point for their supporters.

Although much admiration will be expressed with regard to their leadership qualities, these individuals often tread a solitary path through life and have to be prepared for the appearance of other, equally strong- willed individuals, who will seek to intrude into their sphere of influence. Such people should not be encouraged to linger for there can be only one king or leader in any given environment.

Persons who are subject to this vibration invariably act as a magnet for others who are greatly influenced by the Moon. Such people are especially adept at bringing to fruition the brave new concepts which 'One' individuals initiate and the invaluable assistance they render should never be overlooked, for each requires the other in order to function correctly.

Two

Those whose destiny this is often require a deal of motivation and should seek the company of dynamic individuals - influenced by the Sun - who are currently making their mark on life. Provided that they can ascertain that the aspirations of such people are pure and not motivated by self-purpose, then the 'Two' individuals should become their disciples.

However, they do need to exercise a great deal of caution before committing themselves in such a manner, for their reason for so doing may well stem from an emotional need. Where this occurs, they may well have to absorb some rather bitter lessons en route.

'Two' individuals should be on the alert for the many false prophets currently making their appearance worldwide. These charismatic individuals often commence their activities in a blaze of idealistic fervour but, having feet of clay, all too soon come to believe the many statements made by the sycophants who gather around them.

Whatever they elect to follow these individuals will be very quickly allotted the task of completing or bringing to fruition the most grandiose schemes, for they possess the patience to sift the imponderable and tie loose ends together. Equally their tactful and diplomatic manner can smooth ruffled feathers, encouraging co-operation on many fronts.

In adapting to the wills of stronger personalities they should take care not to fall intro the trap of seeking peace at any price, for that exposes a serious weakness of character. It is not their lot to become the local whipping boy and they have to be prepared to defend themselves, utilising diplomacy to ensure fair play.

Participation within one of the many New Age centres or communities would provide them with the opportunities they require to demonstrate their warm and loving natures, together with their capacitiy to co-operate in schemes for mutual benefit. The influence of the Lady Mary will certainly stimulate their intuitive ability which may then be utilised to great effect within such an environment.

Three

If something is worth doing, it is worth doing well - a valid point to be borne in mind by all those whose destiny this is, and no matter what they aspire to attain or to become during this latter cycle they must learn to think BIG. The combined energies of the planet Jupiter and those of the Venetian Master will provide a constant source of stimulus for their creative abilities during this lifetime. Success can be theirs provided they are prepared to pull out all of the stops and seriously apply themselves to developing and perfecting one particular talent or quality. As all that is worthwhile requires a deal of effort, these individuals should be prepared to burn the midnight oil whilst shaping their destiny.

'Three' people are natural performers, those who can come to enjoy the limelight and hold centre-stage, bringing joy to others by the expression of their charismatic and muti-talented nature. Great popularity will result and they may then be drawn into all manner of social events wherein they will be surrrounded by their many devotees.

Nonetheless they should take care not to be swept away by the adulation, heady as it may be, for their destiny lies within attaining a further measure of growth during the current incarnation.

Four

This is the destiny path of the tactician, scientist, computer programmer or accountant. Those who must follow this are powerfully influenced by Uranus - The Planet of the Will. As a result they will have strong wills which should be used in a constructive manner at all times, demonstrating this by their disciplined use of thought and attention to detail. The vibrational influence of the Ascended Master El Morya will further stimulate them on this level, encouraging the utilisation of the will in a bid to gain entry into one of the many Esoteric Schools He heads world-wide.

To achieve anything of a worthwhile nature during this lifetime, 'Four' individuals need to become hard working and diligent, applying their extremely practical minds to the tasks in hand. A great deal of self discipline may be required which in turn could encourage them to shun social activities, considering these to be a waste of valuable time. In itself this can be an impractical outlook for even machines require a rest and a change of oil from time to time.

Careers which demand precise judgment and accuracy can provide all manner of challenges and their particular skills could be best demonstrated in the fields of engineering, accountancy, architecture or the sciences.

Five

With powerful Mercurial energies influencing all thought and action it may prove difficult for the majority of the 'Five' persons to be still, either mentally or physically. Indeed, Lesson one for those experiencing this vibration: " use words with care - they are valuable".

In this they will be aided by the Master Serapis who endeavours to inspire those who are subject to His vibration with awareness of the necessity for exact and disciplined thinking, particularly influencing those who desire to participate in scientific research.

Despite this, 'Five' individuals will tend to be restless, moving from point to point ever in search of some new sensation - which will invariably be of an illusionary nature. Their popularity will be at an all-time high as the majority of those with whom they mix will be attracted by their quick repartee and seemingly innocuous natures.

Thought begets action and as the thought patterns of these individuals will be somewhat mercurial, their actions will be similarly volatile, making them rather difficult to keep pace with, or to understand. Lesson Two: "Control of thought patterns is imperative!"

To satisfy their wanderlust and seemingly insatiable appetite for new people and experiences they should consider taking up tasks or undertakings which will satisfy these cravings. As they are invariably multi - talented people, possessed individually of a fun personality, a role as a circus clown or travelling entertainer - such as a comic - would satisfy their needs. Failing this, a career as a salesperson could bring them great material benefit, for they could so easily sell the Taj Mahal to the unsuspecting.

As the majority of 'Five' individuals will be drawn to satisfy the human aspect of their natures, they need to beware of over indulgence on this level if an inscription I spotted in New Zealand some years ago is not to become their motto: "Sex is sin. . . but sin is in!" Similarly they should avoid over-indulgence in alchohol and narcotics.

Six

Developing a sense of responsibilty for those with whom they form friendships or relationships - be they of a personal, social, or educational nature - is the key to mastering this particular path of destiny. The influence of the Ascended Master Kuthumi, who as Pythagorus and later as St. Francis of Assisi demonstrated this in the most positive manner, will be both supportive and stimulating.

The influence of the planet Venus which rules this vibration will continually propel 'Six' individuals into situations or undertakings wherein they may express or experience love. These encounters will clearly illustrate the benefits which arise from sharing love for the simple joy this brings about - without any expectation of return. It is this loving of others in a totally unconditional manner which is sometimes referred to as the awakening of Christ Consciousness. This is *THE* lesson for 'Six' individuals.

Others will begin to gravitate towards 'Six' individuals and form into groups around them wherein they will be expected to take on the role of teacher, demonstrating by their loving example the way of the Christ Path.

In their desire to be loved, 'Six' individuals may well accept great responsibilities and offer to assist others with their burdens in life, often without giving due thought to the long term results of such actions. When their physical energies begin to flag, together with their enthusiasm, they may well feel inclined to shed these responsibilites, but should avoid doing so if they wish to retain credibility.

Careers in social welfare, education or spiritual guidance will bring out the best in their nature and they should also utilise their keen sense of colour to create a harmonious environment which will be of benefit to others.

Seven

This path of destiny is marked by the powerful telepathic and visionary powers possessed by those who follow it. These will be further emphasised by the influence of the Ascended Master Rakoczy who appears upon the 7th Ray of Ritual and Ceremony. He will stimulate the consciousness of those who determinedly search for truth and, in return, these individuals will have to play their part as intermediaries between the seen and the unseen. Refusal to accept this role will merely serve to intensify the measure of suffering they undergo, suffering that is in itself borne of their extremely sensitive nature. A measure of joy and happiness can be theirs if they are prepared to investigate the unknown.

The influence of the planet Neptune will also serve to heighten their sensitivity and bring about some unusual psychic experiences. However the human race tends to fear that which it does not truly understand and a fearful nature may well be a characteristic of these individuals. Yet fear in itself is an extemely destructive emotion which can serve to retard the growth of those who indulge in it.

During our formative years we tend to absorb the fears and beliefs of those around and about us. In this manner superstition, ignorance and fear are passed down through the generations. The 'Seven' individual will be expected to overcome these groundless fears and go in search of truth.To this end they should endeavour to develop and utilise their special 'talents of the spirit'.

'Seven' individuals who prefer to develop their mental

powers will find that many opportunities will be presented wherein they may demonstrate these in the practical sciences or in the contemplation of the mystery of life. No matter which path they elect to follow they should at all times endeavour to remain detached, for the mind is but an instrument of communication and they in turn, the intermediary.

The most obvious career for these individual lies within the field of the occult where, with just caution, they may attain their personal destiny in a blaze of illumined thought. Equally, they could select careers in the field of education, the practical sciences, or the church.

Eight

This may prove to be the most difficult of destiny paths to follow and no matter which aspect 'Eight' persons elect to pursue, they must endeavour to become resilient for there are many hard knocks ahead. Saturn - The Great Initiator - governs this vibration, administering justice firmly and frequently in a bid to bring about inner illumination.

The overriding influence of the Lord Maitreya will stimulate hope within those who are subject to it and despite the seemingly impossible with which they will be constantly faced, they can overcome all obstacles and emerge victorious. Acceptance of the inevitable is the key to this challenging vibration. Such acceptance identifies the true initiate.

Materialism and its attendant illusions may well sweep 'Eight' persons off their feet for they could so easily become caught up in the world of business and high finance. Indeed, provided that they can learn to accept the seemingly endless setbacks in a philosphical manner, they can attain a great measure of success. This may be in businesses of their own creation or in heading corporations as dynamic chairpersons, utilising their organisational skills to achieve maximum efficiency.

Where they prefer to follow the inner path in search of illumination and self-purpose, they should be prepared to undergo tremendous rigours of testing and rejection. All that which is worthwhile is marked by enduring efffort and personal sacrifice, and those endeavouring to master this vibration do possess the ability to become New Age Priests.

Nine

This path of destiny marks the culmination of many lives of intense effort. The planet Mars will provide limitless energy, stimulating a great deal of activity for, if there is a goal to achieve or a mountain to climb, 'Nine' individuals will happily accept the challenge. Those whose destiny path this is will succeed only when they are prepared to dedicate their time and energy to helping those in need. The example set by the Ascended Master Jesus - who influences those subject to this vibration - should be emulated wherever possible.

Throughout their lifetime, these individuals will be constantly touched by the predicaments of others and will desire to help alleviate them in some measure. Nonetheless, they must also heed their own physical needs if they are to avoid burning out like fiery meteorites. Little of lasting benefit can be achieved if they damage their physical form in a surfeit of good works. Their overall task lies in setting an example for others to follow.

A career as a doctor or a nurse would prove rewarding, providing them with the necessary opportunities for selfless service, but they may find equal satisfaction in one of the many voluntary organisation. On a personal level, a 'Nine' person should put their artistic abilities to use, for all creative expression which serves to bring colour and harmony into the lives of others provides a valuable healing energy, one which will have untold benefits for those subject to it.

Eleven

Some may assume that the 'Eleven' individuals are blessed with the qualities of genius, as indeed many among them are, but if humanity overall is to put to use all of their highly idealistic ideas, they must be able to demonstrate to all and sundry a practical way in which to bring each and every dream to fruition.

Pluto - the planet of hidden karma - will sorely test the motives of these individuals throughout this current lifetime, dredging up those aspects of the self which they would prefer to keep hidden from view. Throughout life the highly sensitive 'Elevens' will be subject to rejection, as others dismiss their idealistic outpourings as foolish nonsense. Their response to such rejection may be to retreat into a dream world, such action serving to intensify the doubts some may have as to their level of sanity. If they wish to retain this, together with their personal freedom, they must endeavour to remain earthed and practical in outlook.

Those whose destiny this is often receive powerful inspiration of what life on earth could become, for they are deeply intuitive, but need to learn to share such spiritual direction in a down-to-earth manner. Some among them may also possess the gift of prophecy. They should however bear in mind the fact that that such utterances tend to make others feel uncomfortable and the human race is not noted for the kindly treatment of its prophets.

Twenty Two

This is a destiny path guaranteed to test the metal of all who venture upon it. Those who can, at life's end, emerge with a measure of success will be among the few who are proceeding toward self-mastery. Throughout the life great pressures will be brought to bear in a bid to destabilise those who are subject to this vibration and who can expect to be constantly tossed about in the maelstrom of life. The overall goal is to achieve total balance, both within and without the self, which is an extremely difficult undertaking. However, powerful support will be forthcoming from the Ascended Master Djwal Khul who will carefully monitor all humanitarian activity.

Following this pathway are those who, at soul level, desire to become Spiritual Disciples, a task which requires great strength of character and positive leadership qualities. 'Twenty Two's' are natural humanitarians and within one of the world's many voluntary organisations they may endeavour to stir others into action. Possessed of great vision coupled with a practical approach toward life, such individuals can achieve much, if they are so inclined.

Nothing succeeds like success and having proved themselves to be practical visionaries, many powerful and influential individuals may then be drawn to their cause. Sadly, the willingness of such individuals to assist in the fulfillment of a dream arises more from a desire to bask in the light of public acclaim than true idealistic aspiration. Nonetheless, 'Twenty Two's' must be prepared to publicly ackowledge their invaluable support.

Secondary Vibrations

In addition to the aforementioned lessons there are additional testing situations which will affect each and every individual. These are known as the Secondary Vibrations and are hidden deep within the date of birth, acting either as a spur stimulating the person concerned into intense activity, or as an unseen obstacle preventing achievement despite the best of intent.

These Secondary Vibrations are to be found within the sum total of the numerical patterns which influence any particular phase of the life. To gain an insight into what is implied here, let me once again demonstrate with an example. Consider the following date of birth:

15th   January   1929

(Apply a numeric equivalent to the month of birth and where permissable, reduce all numbers to a single digit).

This reduces to: 6   +   1   +   3   Total = 10 = 1

Governing Factor   = 6 - Unconditional Love for mankind.

Personality Factor   = 1 - Independence and leadership.

Maturity Factor   = 3 - Self Expression and expansion.

Destiny Factor   = 1 - Total Independance and positive leadership.

(The latter arising from the intensified 1 energy - (10).

Let us first consider the Governing Factor vibration of 6 which, in addition to playing a formative role during the first twenty eight years of the life, will influence all thought and action throughout the entire lifetime.

From the outset this is likely to be a somewhat emotive incarnation with the need to love and be loved uppermost in this persons mind. This may result in a great expenditure of time and energy in a search for a loving relationship and a number of transitory emotional encounters.

Blind alleys of this nature will serve little purpose for the lesson these people have incarnated to learn lies in learning to love others without any expectation of return. In this manner they may then come to demonstrate a measure of Christ Consciousness. They will also be expected to shoulder all manner of responsibilities within their relationships and this may prove to be a little unpalatable, for the natural inclination of such individuals will be to withdraw whenever such responsibilites become too onerous.

During the first twenty eight years of any lifetime the Destiny Factor vibration also has a part to play in shaping its outcome. The stimulus of this vibration - which exerts a powerful influence on thought and action - has be taken into consideration, in addition to that of the Governing Factor. In this case the Destiny Factor lesson - identified by the number 1 - may stimulate the person concerned to take a responsible role in the home or to seek onerous tasks within their workaday environment (or to avoid same, depending upon their response to this vibration).

In order to locate the Secondary Vibration lesson for the initial stage of this incarnation, we need to take the 1 of the Destiny Factor and add this to the 6 of the Governing Factor, arriving at a Secondary Vibration challenge of 7. This further vibration will play an important role during this early phase of the life, causing the person concerned to respond in a highly sensitive manner to many everyday situations.

As a result, they may emerge somewhat the worse for wear from their many emotional escapades for, due to their extreme sensitivity, they will be easily hurt. They should endeavour to develop the qualities of the Soul which the Secondary Vibration lesson seeks to encourage, learning to follow where their intuition leads them. This ability to attune to Higher Planes of Consciousness could also be put to use to benefit others.

Between the age of 28 and 56 we are subjected to the lesson which the Personality Factor has to teach, although the Governing Factor vibration is still the primary influence on all thought and action. Returning to our example, we note that the Personality Factor lesson also amounts to 1, indicating that a pathway of independent action lies before them, along which a deal of responsibility will come their way.

This is a phase of experience where the personality may express itself in situations which demand responsible leadership (the number 1), undertaken in a loving manner (the number 6), illustrating to onlookers just what can be achieved with determination. However, the Destiny Factor must not be overlooked, for this also influences the whole of the lifetime, beckoning the individual ever forward.

The Secondary Vibration for the central phase of experience amounts to 8 making this an extremely challenging cycle. Governed by Saturn, the number 8 will stimulate a desire to be in control of all situations and people. Where this does not occur they may well decide to withdraw their energy.

This is a very 'earthy' vibration and could well lead to material wealth and power, provided that they can learn to accept the fact that every step along the way will be impeded by all manner of obstacles or restrictions.

If they have mastered the Secondary Vibration of 7 which so influenced the first cycle of experience and developed their intuitive or clairvoyant abilities, they may now call upon these for guidance on how they might best overcome current obstacles. The number 8 also serves to illustrate the inner path and these individuals could well begin metaphysical practices at this time.

During the closing years of life - from the age of 56 onwards, the Maturity Factor lesson of 3 comes into play and this is added to the 6 of the Governing Factor and the 1 of the Destiny Factor to locate the Secondary Vibration lesson for this cycle. Amounting to 10 (which is of course then reduced to a single digit - 1), this serves to intensify the need to lead others in a responsible manner. During this period they need to expand themselves (3) finding expression for their loving nature (6) wherever they may by accepting all responsibility as and when it arises (1).

This exercise may well be a little difficult to grasp and I therefore suggest that you practice this on the following work space.

Work Space

Date of Birth:
Reducing to:

Governing Factor
Personality Factor
Maturity Factor
Destiny Factor

Secondary Vibrations:
Birth to age 28
Age 28 to 56
Age 56 onwards

Conclusion:

One

Here the individual must learn to act independently, accepting whatever responsibility comes along, for there are a great many lessons to be absorbed during this period particularly in the field of leadership. Nothing will be gained by sidestepping such challenges for their task is to prove to others that they have untapped strength, the use of which will surprise many.

These individuals may well fail if they are lazy or stubborn when faced with situations that are not to their liking. They may also be plagued by self-doubt, allowing their fear of failure to cloud their judgement.

Two

Those who are subject to a Secondary Vibration of 2 must learn to become adaptable if they wish to avoid emotional conflict and despair. If they can but learn to bend the knee and accept whatever situation lies before them they will, in surrendering to the Greater Will, overcome! This does not imply seeking peace at any price for that negates growth.

They can become the true power in their environment if they will devote their time and energy to creating an harmonious atmosphere. Here lies a golden opportunity for these individuals to demonstrate their diplomatic skills, while adapting to testing circumstances.

Three

Those who are subject to this Secondary Vibration may respond in a light-hearted manner to everyday responsibilities, either shrugging these aside, preferring illusionary diversions, or withdrawing from the mainstream of life due to a sense of inadequacy.

However, the positive aspect of this vibration can create many oppportunities for these individuals to express the qualities or characteristics which the Primary Vibrations endeavour to stimulate, and they should learn to think and act in the 'grand manner' if they seriously desire success.

Four

This secondary force offers positive assistance to all who are subject to its vibration, encouraging a practical approach toward life. It will also stimulate a desire to succeed and aid the development of a strong character. Indeed this hidden Secondary Vibration could well prove to be a source of strength - one they should try to capitalise upon.

Nonetheless, there are negative aspects to this vibration. These are reflected in resentment when being forced to comply with the will of others, stubborn refusal to cooperate with those about them or outright rebellion against law and order. If their world collapses around them during this cycle, the fault lies with the individuals alone and their tendency to abuse the power of the will.

Five

Although the Primary Vibrations governing this phase of life may indicate a need for restraint and self discipline , this Secondary Vibration may, despite the best of intentions, cause these lessons to be ignored. The mercurial influence of the number 5 will stimulate a desire for freedom and travel and may even encourage irresponsibility. Those who respond in such a manner reflect the negative aspect of this vibration.

Its positive aspect is shown in the development, and expression of their communication skills, light-hearted humour in the face of imponderable odds and mastery of thought and speech.

Six

A need to be loved - stimulated by this Secondary Vibration - will colour all thought and action during this cycle of experience. Major life tasks may well be pushed aside as these individuals search for a loving relationship. However, as they are afraid of commitment they may swiftly withdraw from any relationship which demands this of them.

Although those who are subject to this vibration crave love, they are often unable to express love for others. Until they learn to overcome the desires of their human nature and endeavour to love others - particularly the lost and the lonely - for the simple joy this brings to all concerned, they will continue to feel unloved and unfulfilled.

Seven

Those who are subject to this Secondary Vibration may become exceedingly sensitive, feeling at times that they are mere branches on a tree, being constantly buffeted by the winds of change. Even so, their newly awakened sensitivity may enable them to establish a link with higher planes of consciousness, and the knowledge they gain thereon could enable them to resolve many of life's difficulties.

However, should they respond to the numerous challenges experienced during this cycle in an emotional manner or remain aloof from others, ignoring those situations that call for inspired guidance, then failure may be the result.

Eight

Constant experience of restraint may well cause those subject to this Secondary Vibration to resent the people and the situations they encounter in day to day life. Saturn serves to test their motives and determination here and they need to learn to accept the inevitable without bitterness or rancour.

These individuals should try to see this period as one of opportunity wherein they might refine their characters and bring to the surface the best in their nature. There are no real accidents and if they can but accept this and perceive all that transpires as part of the refining process then they may, like a diamond, emerge to cast light in many directions, the painful cutting and polishing process well behind them.

Nine

No matter which Primary Vibrations influence this segment of life, the Secondary Vibration of 9 will stimulate a desire to aid others and assist the development of their sympathetic nature. Indeed, by channelling their time and energy into good works, they may well master their major lessons with ease. This is a lesson which signifies the end of a cycle of experience, one commenced long, long ago and only a fool will ignore its challenge.

Where they do so and selfishly focus their time and energy upon gratifying the desires of the self, they will fashion an empty and lonely future, for in refusing to aid others, none will wish to assist them in times of need.

Eleven

All who are subject to a Secondary Vibration of 11 should bear in mind that it encourages a tendency to dream, or to retreat - in the face of opposition - to the safety of 'cloud nine'. This is a negative characteristic and should be countered with a determination to locate a practical method of bringing their idealistic concepts to fruition. These individuals are extremely sensitive and very intuitive and this latter quality should be developed to enable them to receive constructive guidance from 'on high'.

Ruled by Pluto, the Planet of Hidden Karma, the 11 vibration will bring all manner of unexpected and unpleasant situations to light. If their response to such situations is to retreat to 'cloud nine', they may well end their days in a secure institution.

Twenty Two

The negative aspect of the 22 Secondary Vibration could well prevent attainment of goals set by Primary Vibrations governing this phase of life. Here the individual may experience a deal of difficulty in making decisions, indeed may defer all decision making, electing to sit on the fence, awaiting a more propitious opportunity. They may also lose sight of their goal in life and be easily swayed by those around and about them.

Countering this indecision will be a desire to dedicate themselves to some humanitarian undertaking, for they do have the vision and practicality of approach required to assist mankind. Although they may well change their opinion constantly and blow hot and cold in their enthusiasms, this vibration will encourage them to strive to attain perfect equilibrium, and so become the master of self. There are alas, very few real successes with this lesson.

Current Year Vibration

Each year of the life brings a fresh challenge for everyone and it is possible to gain an insight into the lesson that lies ahead during that year. This is a relatively simple exercise whereby we add the day and month of our birth together, reducing this where necessary to a single digit, and then replacing the year of the birth with that of the current year.

The Current Year also should be reduced to a single digit and then added to the total reached for the day and month. This may appear a little confusing at first, and as we progress it will be noted that there are certain pitfalls to avoid. Let us consider the following example:

Take a person born on the **14th of March 1940.** Ignoring the year of birth, reduce the 14 to 5 and give the month a numeric identity - ie: 3, and then add these together to reach a sub-total of 8. Now add the numbers which form the year 1995 together. 1 to 9 making 10, plus 9 to make 19 and then the 5. The total of 24 should then be reduced to a single digit of 6.

14th	March	(then insert the current year)	1995
↓	↓	now reduce these to	↓
5	+ 3 = 8		24 = 6

Now add these sub-totals together to find the Current Year lesson.

$$8 + 6 = 14 \text{ (A Danger Signal)} = 5$$

The lesson which lies ahead for this person during 1995 is located in the number 5 - but we must not forget to highlight the Danger Signal of 14 from which this arose.

During 1995, this person will be subject to mercurial mood swings and a great deal of restlessness may eventuate. This in turn could cause them to embark upon world travel, change their job or home, or perhaps both. As a result there may be all manner of dissension in the home. They may also become highly critical of friends and relatives, such criticism being largely of a destructive nature. (This will arise from the influence of the Danger Signal of 14.) Unless they can be constructive in their criticism during this year they would do well to hold their tongue.

On the positive side this will be a year to develop their communications skills, learn a language or expand a talent. With Mercury stimulating thought and speech this could be *the year* in which to impress influential people with their abilities. It will also be a year when they will decide to cast off all that which they have outgrown. This could involve ending relationships, abandoning belief systems or changing careers.

The Current Year cycles are of a *nine year duration* (nine being the number of completion). Pitfalls await the unwary when the overall total amounts to 11 or 22. I have emphasised elsewhere in this book that these numbers should never be reduced to 2 or 4 and then added to other numbers to reach an overall total. However, there are exceptions to every rule and this is the *only* time when this rule is broken.

Consider the following example:

2nd		March		1995	This reduces as follows.
2	+	3	= 5	24 = 6	

When we add these sub-totals together we reach a total of 11 but as the Current Year cycles go no further than 9, we must reduce the 11 to a 2 *but* ensure that in its translation we highlight the idealistic aspect of the year ahead.

Therefore, this individual must be prepared for a somewhat emotional year, one in which they will be expected to bend to the wills of others, adapting to whichever situation presents itself (the influence of the 2). Furthermore, their sensitivity will be heightened throughout the year during which they will receive a great deal of inspiration, serving to stimulate their idealistic concepts for life. However, unless they learn to express their ideals in a down-to-earth manner, illustrating in a practical way just how this may be brought to fruition, they may well suffer a great deal of rejection (the 11).

Where a person was born on the 22nd of November we encounter a similar difficulty. Let me illustrate:

22nd	November	1995	Total
4	(11) = 2	(24) = 6	= 12 = 3

Although the Current Year lesson amounts to 3 we must, in the translation, bear in mind the influence of the two Over-vibrations of 11 and 22. For this person, 1995 will be a year for expansion and growth (3) wherein they may find opportunities to express their high ideals (11) in a practical manner, possibly by becoming involved in some form of humanitarian undertaking (22). I must reiterate however that this is the *only* time in which the two over-vibrations are reduced in this manner.

Workspace

Day and Month of Birth:

Reducing to:

Current Year Lesson:

Overall Lesson for year ahead:

Conclusion:

Day and Month of Birth:

Reducing to:

Current Year Lesson:

Overall Lesson for year ahead:

Conclusion:

One

Those who face this lesson in the year ahead should exercise great caution before committing themselves to any new task, career or relationship. They should ponder at length upon any given situation in order to ascertain that they are fully prepared to spend the next nine years developing this. They should select only those tasks which will enable them to demonstrate their leadership potential and ability to handle responsibility.

They may also begin to exercise a new-found independence in the home, on the work front, or in their social environment. As this is a period of individual challenge, those who are subject to this lesson should, throughout the year, learn to formulate their own ideas and act on their convictions. As a true leader stands alone, they may begin to seek solitude, for detachment aids clear thinking. The downside to this may be that former friends, unable to handle the new positive thrust to their character, may begin to shun them.

There is a need to avoid being drawn into groups or partnerships this year unless they are the majority partner or will play the dominant role. Finally, this will be a year in which a meaningful relationship will be established with a male person who may assist with the development of a new venture. They will remain a positive influence in their life for the remainder of this nine year cycle.

Two

This lesson is the reverse of that experienced during the preceeding year, for the influence of the Moon must be mastered and a need for diplomacy emerges.This will be a year in which those subject to it must be content with slow, progress, for the wills of others will predominate and they would be foolish to refuse to co-operate.

These individuals should keep their particular goals in view and endeavour to impress those in authority with their abilities, particularly their capacity to adapt to constantly changing situations. Above all, this is a year to attend to the minor details which may have been overlooked when making their great leap forward during the preceding year. Failure to attend to these now may lead to a deal of difficulty at a later date.

Many difficult situations will arise this year and the automatic response of these individuals may well be of an emotional nature. As this could prove to be the year for the repayment of karma arising from thoughtless action and abuse of the will during earlier life experiences, they should prepare to be gracious in its acceptance.

Emotions will be running high this year and it is not a good time to launch business ventures for they could easily get their fingers burned. Instead they should utilise the year to develop their latent intuitive ability. With regard to affairs of the heart, romantic links will be somewhat tenuous and care should be exercised in this direction, for there could be many rather than the few - all arising from emotional need.

Three

Having endured the restrictions of the 'Two' year, the 'Three' year will be a joy for it is a year for the experience of many delights. It is certainly not a year in which to choose to be a wallflower for there will be countless opportunities to socialise and become the centre of attention. Social contacts established this year may lead to supportive situations later in the cycle.

Above all, this is a year for self expression and expansion, particularly within the fields of endeavour they explored during the first year of this cycle. Ideas formulated then can now take wing due to the beneficial influence of the planet Jupiter.

As personal popularity could reach new heights during this year, it may result in a number of transitory love affairs but these individuals would be well advised to avoid entering into any long term committments this year for that which is undertaken lightly at this time could well prove irksome at a later date.

This is a year for the release in inner tension and stress and therefore the frivolous and the innane may have a great fascination for these individuals. Despite this they should not overlook the numerous opportunities which Dame Fortune will present - opportunities to demonstrate their multi-talented nature. There is however a need to keep a careful eye on expenditure, both monetary and energy, for both could be utilised unwisely.

Four

A 'Four' year is a challenging one, during which those who experience it must put their shoulders to the wheel and their noses to the grindstone. It will be a year in which they should be prepared to shoulder responsibility and demonstrate their great practicality of approach. They should also endeavour to demonstrate their business acumen, taking care not to express resentment when situations do not work out as they had anticipated.

This is also the time to take a long hard look at past mistakes and the personal weaknesses which may have been responsible for them. These should now be eliminated to ensure that they do not lead to similar problems in the future. It is also a year in which to get everything 'shipshape and Bristol fashion': mental outlook, health, and physical surroundings. Equally, all current relationships, be they of a business or personal nature, must now be placed on a firm footing. Nothing whatsoever should be overlooked, lest it creates imbalance at a later date.

Practical application of energies to business affairs this year will bring great rewards in its wake. However, if these individuals are hoping for a stroke of luck. . . forget it! This is not a year to cast their fate to the winds. Money should be wisely invested and not squandered. Where investment is contemplated, it should be in endeavours which will show a handsome profit at a later date - home improvements, maintaining good health or sound business propositions.

Five

Influence from the planet Mercury will dominate this year and those subject to it will respond in a mercurial manner, with swift changes of mood and opinions, great restlessness and a yearning to travel. If at all possible the latter should be curbed with short journeys to break the monotony. As Mercury also governs the fifth month of May, interesting situations may open up at that time, lasting for a five month period.

Provided that they have heeded the warnings given during the earlier years of this current nine year cycle, these individuals should have their business and social responsibilities well under control and may now take time out to enjoy a measure of freedom. Thought, and its child speech, will be swift this year and creativity will be at its peak. This is the time to grasp all opportunities as they are presented, for these individuals can adapt any given situation to their advantage during this fast-moving year.

This is also the time to sell themselves and their highly individualistic ideas, convincing others of their great potential. They do, of course, require confidence in themselves if they are to convince others and idle boasting will achieve nothing whatsoever. For those who work within small companies or large corporations this is the year to convince superiors that they are ripe for promotion.

Whatever these individuals feel they have outgrown, be it careers, friendships or relationships, they will feel inclined to jettison these this year, particularly that which has become restrictive, for they will find such situations somewhat irksome. It is time for change - and growth!

During the passage of the year, sensual appetites may become unusually intense and being the centre of attention - as they almost certainly will become this year - it could lead to many members of the opposite sex finding their animal magnetism irresistable. Where possible, they should err on the side of caution for the restless mercurial influence may lead to carelessness and those 'accidents' which have a long term outcome. Marriage partners may make their appearance this year or, failing this, close relationships may develop and these could bear fruit during the sixth year of this current cycle.

Six

Those whose year this is will, throughout it's length, be subject to an overwhelming desire to love and be loved. These individuals must ensure that they get their priorities right, endeavouring to develop lasting relationships this year, concentrating in particular on forging friendships that are unconditional in their nature. The emphasis this year will be upon loving others in the purest sense of the word, possibly by undertaking some form of selfless service or by caring for those less fortunate than self.

The influence of the 'Six' year will serve to increase awareness of the necessity to maintain harmony on all fronts, whether in the home, the work front or within relationships of all kinds. Artistic abilities also require an outlet this year and this should be given high priority. This could take the form of introducing a new, harmonious colour scheme into the home environment or by creating a restful garden. These will prove to be invaluable when subject to the influence of the 'Seven' year which is to follow.

This is not a year for embarking upon light-hearted participation in illusionary relationships. These individuals should exercise great care when committing themselves to any course of action, no matter what its nature, for others may have long-term expectations of them. Any committment or under- taking which has now run its course should be brought to a point of conclusion during the passage of the year. Above all, this is a year in which to make long term plans and to be prepared to make whatever adjustments are necessary to effect long-term harmony in all aspects of life.

Seven

This will prove to be a year of great sensitivity, one where those who are subject to its vibrations may well desire to withdraw from the hustle and bustle of life. If so inclined they should take a long hard look at themselves, their current activities and ambition before taking action.

A year in which to bring all thought output under the control of the Higher Self, watchful of those thoughts of an illusionary nature.   Development of the mind is a very definite possibility this year, coupled with in-depth studies of the unknown and contact with higher levels of consciousness.

It is the perfect time to commence the practice of meditation for in stilling the mind they come to know their Higher Self.   This will entail disciplining the lower will and withdrawing from those ego-driven activities which would erve to obstruct such a course of action.

Throughout this year, these individuals should endeavour to rest, taking time out to re-energise their physical form, for the 'Eight' year which follows may prove to be a demanding year. Ideals, goals and aspirations conceived during an earlier part of this cycle may well come to fruition now, provided that they have learned to develop and utilise their mediumistic abilities.

Change is in the air and these individuals may be inclined to initiate it. However they should try to avoid acting on impulse and allow changes to be effected by others. Where change proves to be necessary, it would be wise to delay this until the latter months of the year when the energy of the incoming 'Eight' year will precipitate action.

Eight

The restrictive influence of Saturn will test the metal of those experiencing an Eight year, yet overall it may prove to be an extremely successful year. Saturn, The Initiator, governs this vibration and those who learn to accept the many tests placed upon their path this year will discover that Saturn is also the Great Rewarder.

The dreams and aspirations which they pondered upon during the Seven year should now be put into operation. The mediumistic ability developed during the preceding year may now provide them with positive insights into the future.

Saturn has influence over pecuniary matters and these should prosper this year, with those in business pulling off the unexpected. This is the time to bring to the attention of the general public that which they have striven to perfect throughout this cycle of experience. Provided that this is backed by an efficient organisation and geared to public demand, they could well reap a bountiful harvest.

Although there may be an overwhelming desire to spread their wings this year, they should bear in mind the needs of those less fortunate, and seek to assist those who are not so well organised.

However nothing happens by chance and this will prove to be a year for a deal of hard work. They will need to pay careful attention to detail and to utilise their energies in an efficient manner. It is also the most propitious time to seek out those in authority and to convince them of one's ability and potential. Despite the continual restraint they will experience this year these individuals should hang on to their ideals and strive to attain their personal goals.

Nine

As the planet Mars will influence everything that transpires this year, be prepared for all manner of intense activity. Mars will also have an effect upon the emotional nature and outworn attachments or relationships will be cast aside this year. Nonetheless, be prepared for the brief rekindling of an old love affair.

This is the year to put one's house in order, for it will prove impossible to carry forward anything relating to the current cycle into the one which follows. Emphasis should be placed upon bringing into being original ideas or completing those tasks commenced during this cycle.

All should bear in mind the creative power of thought, for whatever we create within our minds must one day manifest in the world of matter. Better therefore that this transpires whilst we are still aware of its origin and attuned to its energy.

No new plans should be laid or undertakings entered into this year, for they will be lost to view within the rash of new ideas that will be triggered by the incoming cycle. Any undertaking which proved fruitless should now be discarded and the mind cleared of all foolish aspiration. Time now to build upon that which proved to be constructive and successful.

This will also be a year in which to tend to the needs of others, ensuring that this is undertaken in a loving and caring manner. As many demands will be made upon them this year, these individuals should not expend their energy unwisely.

As I have stated at the commencement of this chapter, the Current Year cycles are of a nine year duration, but in the original edition of this book I did include years eleven and twenty two in a bid to highlight situations which do occur. This was incorrect and served only to create confusion in the minds of many of my students. These have therefore been omitted from this edition.

Nonetheless, I do feel that I should include some advice on how to relate to a current year whose component parts initially amount to 11 or 22. Although these numbers have to be reduced to 2 or 4 (the *only* time this must happen) those who are subject to them will respond in quite a different manner from those undergoing a 2 or a 4 year. Take the following example:

$$\text{1st} \quad \text{January} \quad \text{1998}$$
$$1 \quad + \quad 1 = 2 + (27) = 9 \quad \text{Total} = 11$$

Although a year in which emotions will run high and the need for adaptability is paramount, those subject to such energies will be extremely idealistic and emotional levels will be heightened. Tending to shy away from aggressive people or those who reject their idealistic outlook, they may well spend much of this year dwelling on cloud nine, determinedly detached from the world of matter.

If we stop and study the component parts which make up this particular 11 year, we note powerful masculine traits (arising from the 1st of January), which could well serve to stimulate a desire to be down to earth and practical in their outlook, with a strong determination to lead mankind where others fear to tread. In this pattern therefore there is a great potential for success, provided that those subject to this intensified lesson are prepared to accept the will of those around and about them.

A situation where the influence of a Twenty Two could affect the outcome of a Current Year is more difficult to locate, but perhaps we could consider the following .

2nd		September			2009	
2	+	9	=	11	+ 11	Total = 22

In reducing this to a 4 to fit in with the Current Year patterns, do not lose sight of the influence of the two '11's and the 22, for they will serve to influence all thought and action. The two seperate sub-totals of 11 make this a year for extreme sensitivity and these individuals will need to be extremely earthed if they are to retain their sanity. The influence of the 22 will encourage participation in all manner of humanitarian undertakings this year, but there needs to be an underlying practicality of purpose in all which they undertake. Willpower may also be extremely strong and this should be harnessed wisely, avoiding the tendency to ride roughshod over others in a grim determination to achieve a desired goal.

The Power In Your Name

Having reached an understanding of the various lessons located within the date of birth, further challenges await, hidden from view within the various names we bear. Far from being a whim of the parents, the names which a child is given are inspired by Higher Minds. What is more, each name has a specific meaning - a fact long acknowledged within ancient civilisations.

Forenames are intended to identify a particular pathway which each soul should endeavour to follow through life. Take for instance the name Edmund. This means 'Rich Protector' - a role I studiously avoided until I reached the age of thirty three. Having finally accepted - and adopted this in my daily life - its greater purpose was revealed.

For those who wish a more detailed knowledge of this fascinating subject may I suggest that they take the time to study one of the many books which deal specifically with the meanings of names.

Returning to the subject of numerology, each individual name has hidden within it certain numeric patterns and these do have a part to play in the outcome of the lifetime. Where any person is blessed with a number of forenames, the various (often conflicting) energies serve to create an extremely complicated personality.

Some people tend to make their life much more difficult by altering their names in the vain belief that they may escape their original life lesson. Sadly such hope is doomed to failure, for we can at best but accentuate the positive therein by the act of amending or taking on another name. The original lesson, alas, must still be absorbed.

The lessons within the names we bear are secondary in importance to those found within the date of birth, but should not be overlooked. When seeking to locate these additional lessons, the numerologist must always work on the names shown on the birth certificate. Any amendments thereto by deed-poll or marriage must be viewed seperately, for they reflect another lesson which that individual has elected to carry through life.

The only exception to this rule lies within a case of adoption when the numerologist should work on the names given by the adoptive parents, although the original name may serve to provide an insight into why the individual responds in certain ways to everyday events.

When correctly charted, the name will reveal personal characteristics and possible reaction to given situations. Three major lessons are found within the name, these being:

Spiritual Purpose: representing the path of the Higher Self.

Egoic Desire: reflecting the challenge for the Lower Will.

Overall Self-Expression: indicating the manner whereby both aspects of the self may be best expressed.

Before commencing, it will be necessary to create a simple chart as follows.

1	2	3	4	5	6	7	8	9
A	B	C	D	E	F	G	H	I
J	K	L	M	N	O	P	Q	R
S	T	U	V	W	X	Y	Z	

The first task lies in becoming familiar with the numbers allocated to each letter of the alphabet. Note for instance that the letters A. J. and S all relate to the number 1, whilst E. N. and W. all correspond to the number 5 and so on. Once you are able to relate to the letters of the alphabet in this manner you will no longer need to refer to a chart.

Taking this one stage further let us create another chart. Place the numbers which correspond to the *vowels* within the name on a line *above* and those which relate to the *consonants* should be entered *below* . It is also important to reduce the numeric patterns appertaining to each segment of the name to a single digit, as shown below . This is to ensure that any Over-Vibration is not overlooked.

$$20 = (2) \quad + \quad 10 = (1) \quad \text{———} \; = \quad 3$$
$$51 \quad 9 \; 5 \qquad\qquad 9 \quad 1$$

BEATRICE **McMILLAN**

$$2 \quad 29\,3 \qquad\quad 4\,34\,33 \quad 5$$
$$16 = (7) \quad + \quad\quad (22) \qquad \text{———} \; = \quad 22 + 7$$

(Using the 22 as a denominator, add the 3 to the 7 to arrive at the Overall Self Expression lesson). $= \quad 22 + 1$

Spiritual Purpose	=	3	= Self Expression
Egoic Desire	=	22 + 7	= Practical Visionary
Overall Self-Expression	=	22 + 1	= Humanitarian leadership

Let us consider the example shown above. Vowels within the name relate to the pathway which the Higher Self has incarnated to follow. This I refer to as the **Spiritual Purpose**. The numbers set out above the name corresponding to the vowels therein amount to a grand total of 3. The Higher Self must therefore seek some form of expression during this lifetime, which will in turn lead to spiritual expansion and growth.

Consonants serve to identify the challenge which the

Lower Will (or Ego) must face throughout the lifetime. This is known as the **Egoic Desire** lesson. In this example we encounter a major challenge, one which is overlooked by those who add all numbers together in a bid to reach an overall total. In so doing they overlook vital pointers which the Over-Vibrations of 11 and 22 serve to illustrate.

Where 22 or 11 appear as a sub-total they must *never* be added to the remaining numbers, but used to highlight the lesson. Here the Egoic Desire is shown to be 22 + 7. (No matter where an Over-Vibration appears in name or date of birth, it must always be identified as the primary vibration and used as a denominator).

The Ego will desire to locate self-expression within some form of humanitarian undertaking (22) wherein the intuitive or clairvoyant faculty (7) may be utilised to great effect. However it should be borne in mind that the Ego is the Lower Will and may not desire to co-operate with the Higher Self in any manner. As the result it may encourage fence sitting throughout the life, avoiding decisions wherever possible (the negative aspect of 22), and responding in an overly-sensitive manner to everyday events (the negative aspect of the number 7).

Had we followed the practice suggested by some schools of thought and overlooked the Over-Vibration of 22, by simply adding all of the consonants throughout the name together, we would have reached a grand total of 11 (another Over-Vibration) and further reduced this to 2. To then advise the individual concerned that they must adapt to changing situations and avoid overly emotional responses would be totally incorrect and misleading.

The last of these three lessons is known as the **Overall Self-Expression** vibration and this relates to that by which we are recognised by all and sundry - the outer manifestation of the total self if you wish. This identifies the pathway upon which both aspects of the self may find the greatest form of expression. To arrive at this we add the Spiritual

Purpose and Egoic Desire lessons together. Normally this would present no difficulty, but as an Over-Vibration occurs within the Egoic Desire lesson we must practice great caution.

As we may not add the 22 to any other number, we again utilise this as a denominator for the Overall Self-Expression lesson and then add the 7 of the Egoic Desire to the 3 of the Spiritual Purpose to make 10 and then reduce this to 1. Thus we identify the Overall Self Expression lesson as 22 + 1. Both aspects of the self may find expression within some form of humanitarian undertaking (22) wherein our subject's highly individualistic form of leadership (the intensified 1) may be called upon to bring about much that will be to the benefit of humanity.

The keen-eyed among my readers will have noticed the Danger Signal 16 in the sub-division of the figures appertaining to the consonants in the forename of our subject. This has been ignored for it has no part to play in our translation. However, had the final addition of these numbers amounted to 16, we would most certainly have highlighted this when sharing the information with the person concerned.

Study the various lessons which follow and then put these into practice on the Work Space.

Work Space

1	2	3	4	5	6	7	8	9
A	B	C	D	E	F	G	H	I
J	K	L	M	N	O	P	Q	R
S	T	U	V	W	X	Y	Z	

Vowels

Name:

Consonants

Spiritual Purpose   =

Egoic Desire   =

Overall Self-Expression =

Concise translation:

Spiritual Purpose

From time to time we will all be drawn to take up those challenges which the Higher Self desires to experience, even though these may conflict with other vibrations governing our lives. Such is our Spiritual Purpose. The journey through this world of matter brings a wealth of experience via which the Soul attains its desired measure of growth.

One

Under this vibration the Higher Self desires to set the pace and no matter what task is undertaken, all actions will be strongly self-orientated. The challenge here lies in learning to lead others by the power of example and not by the use of the will. The negative aspect of this vibration may encourage them to (mistakenly) assume that they have the capacity to overcome each and every challenge. This over-confident outlook may well cause them to air their knowledge to all and sundry or to publicly demonstrate their skills in an egoic manner.

Although independence is something these individuals will determinedly pursue, they will from time to time crave the approbation of others. This can prove to be dangerous, for they will attract more than their fair share of sycophants. If they are to avoid rejection and some rather bitter lessons en route, they should learn to encourage others to fulfil their own personal goals, even where these run counter to their own.

Two

Whilst the stimulating energy of the number 1 may have encouraged headstrong responses, this vibration seeks to encourage the reverse. Here the Spirit Self must experience the spiritual backwaters, moving only in those directions permitted by the tide of public opinion. Nonetheless there will be ample opportunity to be still and take stock of the self, whilst attempting to develop tactful and diplomatic responses to those around and about them.

With regard to spiritual endeavours, these individuals may find their path blocked by others who will demand that they abandon their preferred pathway (or beliefs) and follow where they lead. However, if they will but learn to listen to the still, inner voice, they will then receive inspiration on how to respond to such situations.

Three

The irresponsible aspect of the nature may surface here and as there will be a strong desire to be in the limelight, care must be taken not to abuse the spiritual talents merely to gain a measure of notoriety. Those who follow this pathway should consider taking up the practice of meditation in a bid to discipline the lower mind and to tap into the storehouse of the Higher Mind. Long-forgotten knowledge may then resurface and be used to benefit mankind. These individuals may however flit from belief to belief, or teacher to teacher, avoiding thereby their spiritual responsibilities. If they squander their opportunities in this fashion during the present incarnation, future life experiences may prove to be difficult as a consequence.

Four

Whilst the lighthearted 'Three' vibration encourages the enjoyment of life, that of the 'Four' may result in the rejection of all that is illusionary in favour of the practical. Rigidity of outlook, particularly with regard to beliefs, family, and pastimes often identifies these individuals, who will demand unquestioning loyalty from loved ones and close friends. Many who undergo this lesson are to be found among the dour stalwarts of some religions, dogmatic in their utterances and unwilling to even consider different concepts of belief.

These individuals invariably lack a sense of humour and can often become 'kill-joys', making life arid for themselves and those about them. They have to learn that there must be a measure of leavening to make life palatable and that a sense of humour is an essential part of the make-up of the would-be initiate. A very strong will is certain to be evident and this must be brought under control, for if it is utilised to dominate others they may well rue the day.

Five

A relatively happy experience lies ahead of those who are subject to this vibration, for the freewheeling 'Five' energy will bring about an ease of communication, resulting in a measure of popularity. There will also be a strong desire to travel. A sense of humour - so sadly lacking in those subject to the Four vibration - comes to the fore to assist these indviduals to see the humorous side of the more difficult situations they will encounter in life.

This vibration also encourages the expansion of mental faculties, governed as it is by the planet Mercury. Detailed study of esoteric subjects may well prove to be irksome for some who may find them time consuming. Yet if they will determinedly discipline the restless lower mind, they may gradually receive direction from the Higher Self. This could then result in a spiritual quickening, and eventually their assuming the mantle of the teacher.

Creative skills may also be at an all-time high and should be expressed wherever possible, for these too are a reflection of the evolution of the Soul.

Six

The Soul which elects to master this vibration has incarnated in a bid to develop and express a measure of Christ Consciousness, whereby they love everyone equally, such love being devoid of all expectation. This may result in a determination to defend the 'under-dog' or to become 'knights in shining armour', fighting against injustice.

However there should be no ulterior motive, and such acts should only be undertaken from the standpoint of ensuring fair-play. Where such tasks are accepted in the hope that they will be loved in return, these individuals may well be disappointed. Although it is human to desire to be loved, the challenge presented by this vibration is to endeavour to rise above physical needs and to reflect the higher, spiritual nature.

Seven

Due to a hyper-sensitive nature those who experience this vibration may well shun the world, preferring the seclusion of the countryside. Yet that very sensitivity can prove to be their greatest asset. Reflecting as it does, the feminine side of their dual nature, this quality should be developed to enable them to bypass the illusions of this Plane of Matter and the Astral Realm and to attune to the Higher Planes of Consciousness. Here they may gain insight into future world events, or tap into a vast storehouse of knowledge. The purpose of the Soul which incarnates to master this vibration is to endeavour to become a clear spiritual vessel, one which may then be called upon by Higher Minds to act as their intermediary.

For some, filled with all manner of fears, real or imaginary, a religious way of life may have a powerful attraction , the world of the occult being deeply repellent for them. Others may prefer to develop their intellect and find expression within the practical sciences. Such individuals often select their friends with care, surrounding themselves with others of like mind.

Eight

The Spirit faces a tremendous adversary here in that Saturn which governs this vibration will encourage the pursuit of monetary gain and power, whilst the Higher Self prefers to follow the path of self discipline and initiation (also encouraged by Saturn). No matter which path they elect to follow - and much will depend upon the nature of the Governing Factor and Destiny Factor influences here - these individuals will encounter all manner of restraint or restriction throughout their life. Yet it is only through continuous and rigorous testing that they will find success, on either level. So in the tradition of the scout movement they should 'always be prepared' for the inevitable.

Where they can bring themselves to accept all adversity as a necessary part of their growth pattern, the Soul will then progress and a measure of success is assured. If however, they become bitter and resentful cursing their lot in life, then they will fail and may then have to endure a number of health problems, for negative thinking of this nature will result in all manner of painful diseases!

Nine

Here the Higher Self seeks to complete a spiritual undertaking commenced during an earlier lifetime. These individuals will need to learn to husband their Martian energy for unwise depletion of physical energy levels (often in caring for others) may lead to ill health later in life. This point cannot be stressed too strongly, for these caring individuals have difficulty in saying "No" when faced with need in others. They are invariably caring, dedicated and talented people and are among the world's great benefactors.

The purpose for incarnation is to seek experience of the world of matter and to grow spiritually by overcoming the pull of illusion, and the swiftest method of attaining this goal is through selfless service to mankind. The negative aspect of this vibration encourages self interest and selfish activities, both of which will serve to defeat life's purpose.

Eleven

The Higher nature is much to the fore upon this vibration, encouraging the desire to resolve many of the worlds's ills. Sadly, a practical approach is often lacking and these individuals may suffer continual rejection until they learn to present their idealistic propositions in a constructive manner. Dismissal of their well-intentioned proposals may result in their withdrawing from life, content to exist in a dream world where everything is perfect. Such reactions could possibly lead to insanity.

In a bid to overcome mankind's natural responses to their idealistic fervour, these individuals should pay serious attention to the expansion of their intuitive faculty, determining to bypass all illusionary planes of consciousness. They may then become intermediaries between the seen and the unseen and, provided that they request this, they will begin to receive practical guidance for the human race.

Twenty Two

Here the Higher Self will seek to activate humanitarian ideals and as those who are subject to this vibration are possessed of a practical nature, much progress can be made during this incarnation. These individuals will be drawn to serve within organisations whose energies are dedicated to resolving the problems which beset the human race. Possessing both the vision and the will to succeed they may well emerge to the fore, there to play a part in the resolution of international problems.

This is a challenging vibration, one which helps to fashion the Spiritual Disciple. These individuals will be expected to demonstrate in a quiet, resourceful manner how they come to terms with the many petty tyrannies to which they will be subjected. Total equilibrium is called for at all times, no matter what the nature of the conflict around and about.

They should however exercise caution when offered powerful positions for such roles can corrupt even the most idealistic among us, laying to waste thereby even the best laid of plans. Many may find this vibration all too difficult and sit on the fence for much of their lives, skilfully avoiding all decisions.

Egoic Desire

Consonants within the names we bear relate to the Ego or Lower Will and the lesson this aspect of the self is here to learn. Until the moment when the will of Higher Self begins to manifest, directing attention to the spiritual pathway, the Lower Will is given free reign and the personality develops, mistakenly assuming that it is the *whole* self. It will therefore strive to block the will of the Higher Self, obstructing wherever possible, any action that runs contrary to its desire.

One

The lesson here lies in developing a positive and vigorous personality and determinedly seizing independence. Those subject to this lesson should also grasp every possible opportunity to express their highly original ideas, for the world is their oyster - and the world loves a winner!

There is little that these individuals cannot achieve with determination, for leadership and responsibility come naturally to them. However, on their way to the top, these individuals should learn to cultivate loyal friendship, for if their ideas do not produce the expected results, they may need supportive friends on their way down.

Should they reject all proffered opportunities to play a responsible role in society, clinging weakly to others for support, or where they seek to dominate weaker-willed persons, these individuals reveal a weakness of character and reflect the negative aspect of this vibration.

Two

'Two' Personalities have to learn to adapt to the will of those around them, a difficult task which will require a deal of diplomatic skill. A measure of success may come about when they learn to place their own desires aside and apply their energies to transforming the aspirations of others into practical concepts. Peace and harmony is the keynote here - but not peace at any price!

Not for them worldly dreams or powerful positions, but the role of the peacemaker, focussing love in abundance upon those within the family unit or close friends. The emotional nature will dominate. The pinpricks of everyday life often too much to bear. Mastery of their runaway emotions is vital if they are to experience any measure of joy.

Three

A deep desire to leave their imprint upon life identifies the 'Three' Personality. Bright, charming individuals, much given to the enjoyment of 'the good life' and often noted at the centre of social activities expressing their points of view. The planet Jupiter governs this vibration encouraging an appreciation of beauty and worldly possessions.

It is a vibration to enjoy, and those subject to it should utilise this opportunity to expand their personality. In addition they should also take the time to express the deeper, spiritual aspect of their nature, or perfect one of their obvious talents. Those who ignore all opportunities for expression and who refuse to develop their latent talents, may develop a cynical outlook upon life and a jaundiced view of spiritual purpose.

Four

A strong willed personality emerges upon this vibration with a tendency toward stubbornness and rebellion against authority. These are reflections of the negative aspect of this vibration and should be overcome if they desire a measure of happiness. On the positive front they can be hardworking, and responsible individuals. They do need to watch the tendency to become workaholics and of having the same expectancy of others!

Possessed of practical natures they should channel their energies into business undertakings for there could be the opportunity to build empires, both large and small. A tendency toward miserliness is another negative trait encouraged by the lower aspect of this vibration and these individuals should bear in mind the fact that money is an energy , one which they should use wisely.

'Four' Personalities tend to be wary of emotional display whether in private or in public and may have difficulty in relating to others emotionally. This weakness may rob them of many of the simpler joys in life.

Five

Illusions of every kind will act as a magnet for the 'Five' Personalities, particularly those which they studiously avoided during the preceeding cycle. The unknown will hold a great fascination, particularly the uncharted depths of their own emotional nature. As their popularity levels will be high - as will their animal magnetism - a deal of experimentation of a sensual nature may result.

These individuals will be restless with a deep dislike of

any form of restraint. They may also sidestep all forms of responsibility, considering these to be restrictive. There may also be a ruthless tendency to discard anything they consider to have outlived its usefulness, including friends, associates and lovers.

In order to achieve the measure of expansion which the personality seeks during this incarnation, they would be well advised to focus their attention upon developing one of their diverse talents, particularly one which may be of benefit to humanity.

Six

With Venus ruling this vibration, a deal of emphasis will be placed upon loving and being loved and those subject to it may seek affection in fleeting and illusionary relationships. As certain aspects of this vibration can arouse the element of the philanderer, the 'Six' Personalities will need to maintain strict control over their emotional nature. The real challenge here lies in learning to rise above sensuality or possessiveness and to find joy in loving others without expectation of return.

Some who undergo this lesson may be considered 'busybodies', forever interfering in the affairs of others, particularly when they sense deliberate manipulation of weaker individuals. However, such actions will be based on the purest of motives for they will feel impelled to act to ensure fair play and justice for all.

Seven

Neptune governs this vibration and its influence is reflected in a highly sensitive personality which may respond to everyday events in an emotional manner, or taking offence where none is intended.   The fact that many 'Seven' Personalities are quite psychic may cause others to be wary of them, such reactions serving to increase their sense of isolation. This can lead to their retreating from the harsh realities of the physical world into a mental 'ivory tower'. If they wish to retain their hold on sanity they   should   control this tendency.

They have the potential to become benefactors of the race, utilising their uncanny abilities to guide or direct those who are lost or confused. Provided that they do so in a down-to-earth manner and do not deliberately set out to create an air of mystique , they will gradually become accepted. A sense of humour would be a decided advantage, particularly as they will be called upon to make a sacrifice or a personal nature at some time during this incarnation.

Eight

If any vibration could be said to aid the acquisition of material wealth it is that of the number 8 , for it is influenced by the planet Saturn which has dominion over monetary matters. Nonetheless it will not be an easy victory for Saturn is known as the Great Initiator bringing a multitude of restrictive situations into being in order to test the mettle of those subject to His influence. If the 'Eight' individuals can learn to smile in the face of adversity, taking all obstacles in their stride and accepting restraint as a necessary proving ground, then they will succeed where others fail. Nonetheless, success will only come about if they are prepared to work extremely hard in order to attain their goal.

Wealth and power often go hand in hand and those who acquire them also experience a deal of popularity as selfseekers endeavour to grasp a portion of their abundance. However all material wealth and possessions are illusionary, to be left behind at some point in time, and these individuals would be wise to apportion part of their hard-earned gains to those who can put it to good use for the benefit of others. Mastering these powerful illusionary forces is the greatest challenge 'Eight' Personalities will face during this difficult life experience.

Nine

Throughout this incarnation 'Nine' Personalities will feel compelled to complete any given task to the best of their ability, frequently pushing themselves beyond the limits of physical endurance. As Mars rules this vibration, all who are influenced in any way by the number 9 should learn to take note of their physical energy levels, taking frequent breaks in order to restore these. Many of course may ignore such warnings considering it to be a sign of weakness to rest. Responses of this nature arise from a stubborn refusal to accept defeat and where they become a habit, major health problems may eventuate.

The overall lesson for these personalities lies in completing a task commenced during an earlier life cycle and this is best accomplished by following their natural bent and volunteering to assist those less fortunate than self. 'Nine' people are often to be found playing supportive roles within voluntary organisations, be it church committees, union branches or political bodies. However their artistic talents should not be overlooked for these can also be utilised to enrich the lives of others.

Eleven

'Eleven' Personalities tend to be highly idealistic in outlook and extremely sensitive to public opinion. This is a vibration with a low success rate, for few among them take the time to fashion their high ideals into practical propositions which may be appreciated by all. Invariably strong willed - with a marked reluctance to change their opinions once they have reached a decision - they tend to retreat to their favourite cloud to sit in judgement on those who dared to reject their propositions.

Pluto the Planet of Hidden Karma influences all who are subject to this vibration and these individuals should prepare themselves for a number of unpleasant surprises as hidden aspects of their natures surface. Karma cannot be sidestepped and these personalities must endeavour to accept such situations with a brave face and not retreat to cloud nine.

Twenty Two

Those who incarnate to experience this, the most challenging of vibrations, should endeavour to strive for balance at all times, taking time out to be still when conflict swirls around them. With friends and loved ones demanding their support on opposing fronts, it will be all too easy for 'Twenty Two' Personalities to withdraw from a position at the centre of life and sit on the sidelines, avoiding all decisions.

Those among them who do determine that they will not be dissuaded from their goals may then find expression for their practical idealism within an organisation dedicated to some humanitarian purpose, often emerging at its head. They should however be ever mindful of the fact that success and popularity breed jealousy among powerful people.

Overall Self Expression

This lesson arises from the combination of the Spiritual Purpose and Egoic Desire vibrations and presents an opportunity for each individual to express both aspects of the self on yet another front.

One

Here both aspects of the self combine to find expression within dynamic action, for 'One' individuals must be bold and positive, prepared to assume the mantle of authority and take control of those everyday situations which call for positive action. Provided that they have faith in their ability to succeed, they can achieve the seemingly impossible which in turn will offer much needed encouragement for those who follow in their footsteps.

Others will be observing events from the sidelines waiting to see the outcome of events and the 'One' individuals must be prepared to lead by the power of their example if they wish to succeed. In addition they will require endless patience when dealing with those whose task it is to carry out their commands, some of which may not always be practical.

The pioneering spirit will be much to the fore during this lifetime and these individuals may well embark upon many new and exciting ventures. If they can combine Higher Self aspiration with three-dimensional ambition they may bring about harmonious co-operation between both aspects of the self.

Two

This may well prove to be an extremely emotional lifetime, for it is greatly influenced by the Moon and these individuals may be surrounded by exceptionally strong willed people. If this is to be a tolerable incarnation, they will have to learn early in life to adapt to the dictates of others, developing a diplomatic response to everyday events. Being naturally sympathetic to the predicaments of others they would do well to pursue a career in social welfare which would provide ample expression for their sensitive and caring natures.

As leadership is not their particular forte, 'Two' individuals are best suited to the role of second-command, aiding more dominant personalities to fulfil their tasks. In such positions they will soon prove to be invaluable, tying together the loose ends often overlooked by their supervisors.

Three

The powerful energies of Jupiter will encourage these individuals to sidestep their responsibilities putting off all decisions for another day, viewing life as they do in a light-hearted manner. With rarely a thought of what tomorrow may bring they prefer the social life, wherein they will find a deal of popularity. These individuals will be able to charm the birds out of the trees, and this characteristic may stand them in good stead when seeking to gain the attention of influential people.

The reverse side of this vibration encourages them to become 'shrinking violets' who avoid all social contact. As they do possess a number of latent skills or talents, they should devote time to perfecting one of these rather than becoming a Jack (or Jill) of-all-trades.

Four

Those who incarnate for this experience should bear in mind that the human body - in common with a well maintained machine - must rest from time to time, as a workaholic metality may prevail. Extremely conventional in outlook these individuals are not the type to make rash decisions but will seek to use their powerful will when faced with opposition. They should seek careers which allow them to freely express their practical nature and are best suited to trades/professions which demand concentration and accuracy.

Material security is very important to 'Four' people and there may be a tendency to hoard all manner of rubbish and to be rather miserly. However, money in common with all forms of energy must be allowed to flow freely if long term benefits are to accrue - a suggestion likely to be ignored by most 'Fours'.

Five

Great communication skills are possessed by those who are subject to this vibration. These should be developed, perfected and channelled into a suitable environment. The world of theatre or dance may be perfect for some, whilst radio, televison, or the media in general would be more suitable for others. These individuals should also consider creative advertising, a field wherein they could excel.

They will never be at a loss for words, their silver tongues and quick repartee evoking gales of laughter (or shouts of rage when the response is unkind). Quick witted and mercurial by nature they live for the moment rather than a nebulous tomorrow. They should avoid indulging in petty gossip or empty boasting for both will be to their detriment.

Six

A caring nature and a desire to be loved will be very evident within these people and the latter could well mar their life with much time spent in the pursuit of a loving relationship. There will also be a strong desire for justice and fair play. As there will also be a strong desire to champion the under-dog, they should select a career wherein these characteristics may be best expressed. As they may feel stifled in certain environments, they should ensure that their chosen career will permit them a measure of freedom of thought and expression.

Management levels within governmental services, particularly those dealing with international aid programmes or education would prove stimulating, as would the medical field or social welfare. In such a workaday environment they will be given many opportunities to love without expectation of return - their major challenge in life!

Seven

Many who experience this vibration lead unhappy lives for they are little understood by those around and about them, a fact not always aided by an aloof manner. Possessed of a deeply sensitive nature, their natural inclination is to retreat from life, being uncomfortable when surrounded by large numbers of people.

Nonetheless, they are gifted individuals, blessed with the ability to communicate with Higher Minds and Planes of Consciousness. Some among them also have the capacity to readily identify the talents possessed by others, thus encouraging them to fulfil their true purpose in life. This skill is best channelled into the role of Spiritual Counsellor, whereby they may utilise their sixth and seventh senses to the highest degree.

If such undertakings fill them with apprehension or fear they should perhaps develop the analytical aspect of their nature and seek a career within the field of psychology or psychiatry. As 'Seven' individuals also have a deep affinity with the world of nature, market gardening, rare plant cultivation or landscaping could well satisfy their needs.

Eight

If anyone can achieve worldly success it has to be 'Eight' individuals; shrewd characters who have the necessary ambition, drive and grim determination to get to the top. These qualities are enhanced by the influence of Saturn, which will encourage the pursuit of material wealth. Big business will certainly beckon and, provided that they are astute in their business dealings, success just has to be around the corner.

The generally held view of these individuals is that they are quite ruthless, fully determined to reach the top in their chosen profession. However success will not be easily attained and their journey through life will be marked by a series of conflicts, obstacles, even a minor disaster or two, until they learn to take everything in their stride. The major lessons for those experiencing this lesson lie within coming to terms with restraint, wealth and power.

Nine

Those who have selected this lesson should grasp the golden key of opportunity and devote themselves to caring for others, for the greatest measure of growth (which is the purpose of incarnation) is to be found within selfless service to their fellow men and women. Any career which offers free reign to humanitarian impulses will bring great satisfaction, particularly the field of medicine wherein they will be faced with many a testing situation which will aid personal growth. General nursing and organisations devoted to animal welfare will also hold a strong attraction.

These people will have explosive temperaments and should endeavour to keep this negative trait under firm control, for it could well undo all the good created by their selfless acts. They should also be watchful of their physical energy levels, taking the time to rest when exhaustion sets in. Failure to do so, often due to a stubborn determination to complete a task within a given time frame, may lead to serious health problems.

Eleven

Those subject to this vibration are often great visionaries who desire to improve the quality of life world-wide. Decidedly idealistic, they must strive to make their dreams practical, illustrating a constructive method whereby these may be put into operation. Failure to do so is almost certain to guarantee rejection by all and sundry.

'Eleven' individuals are invariably possessed of strong wills, matched only by their determination to stick to their guns in the face of stiff opposition. Should this become a habitual practice it could lead to painful arthritic conditions later in life.

Any career which demands an imaginative approach and natural creativity will provide them with a great deal of personal satisfaction, particularly if drawn to those professions which deal in illusion, such as the theatre or the cinema. The world of dance, choreography, set design or the instruction of others in philosophical pursuits would be ideal for them.

Twenty Two

People who must undergo this experience should endeavour to emulate those who constructed the pyramids, for they too should set out to create something which will be to the lasting benefit of mankind. A rather tall order for most 'Twenty Two' individuals and possibly the reason why most fail. However they have in earlier life experiences developed a practical approach to idealistic concepts, and reappear at this point in time to put them into practice.

As they will need to capture the imagination of mankind, particularly with regard to humanitarian undertakings, they should endeavour to activate their natural intuitive ability, calling upon this when faced with all manner of challenges. These individuals can certainly acquire a measure of power and glory, just so long as they are prepared to fight to retain it! Balance is the key to this life experience, something they will be hard pressed to retain.

The Dynamics of Self

The various numbers allocated to the letters which make up the names we bear could be said to represent the genetic factors of our whole being or the dynamics of the self. These serve to indicate a person's potential together with the weaknesses to which all are prone. Having dealt with the major patterns located within the name, there are other patterns to which I wish to draw to your attention. These being

    (a) **Inspirational Capacity:**   (b) **Mental Power:**
    (c) **Physical Strength**   (d) **Vital Force:**

The first pair of numbers (A & B) may be considered to be of lesser importance but close attention should be paid to C & D particularly when endeavouring to ascertain the cause of physical weariness. There appears to be no logical reason as to why these combinations of numeric energies influence different aspects of our being, but speaking from personal experience, I have found them to be amazingly accurate. Consider the following:

```
     5 1      9 5            9   1
     B E A T R I C E    Mc M I L L A N
     2     2 9   3       4 3 4   3 3     5
```

Inspirational Capacity	(7 & 9)	= 3
Mental Power	(1 & 8)	= 2
Physical Strength	(4 & 5)	= 5
Vital Force	(2:3: & 6)	= 6

In this exercise we are looking at *how often* the various numbers appear, seeking a ratio as it were in a bid to ascertain how this person will respond to specific situations in life. We will begin with the first pair of numbers. Ignoring where they appear (be it above or below the name) ascertain *how many times* the numbers seven and nine appear. The number nine appears three times, the number 7 not at all. We then repeat this exercise to see how often the numbers one and eight appear. The number one appears twice and the number eight not at all.

With a ratio of three to two, our subject has a greater *Inspirational Capacity* (although the difference is not marked) and she will tend to rely more upon her intuitive ability than to use her mental capacity. Therefore her response to most situations encountered in daily life would be fairly swift, although possibly illogical to some observers

As I have noted above, the difference between these abilities is not great and this individual does have a practical mind when she cares to apply it. However, it would always be far easier for her to act on intuitive impulse than to work things out in a logical manner. In following her inner guidance she will rarely put a foot wrong, for this is a quality of the Spirit Self.

The final pair of numbers are of greater importance in that they serve to forewarn of possible physical weakness. The numbers four and five relate to the *measure of strength* within the physical form and these appear five times - the number 4 twice and the number 5 three times. This indicates that our subject has a fairly strong physical body but we must now ascertain her vitality levels by checking how frequently the numbers two, three and six appear. The answer is six.

Once again the measure of difference here is not great, but it should serve as a warning to the person concerned. Her vitality level being the greater, will encourage her to approach most physical tasks with a great deal of enthusiasm. This may well result in our subject pushing her physical form beyond its limits of endurance, and collapsing from sheer exhaustion. Although her physical form is quite strong, if this person were to ignore these warning signs, then this could result in serious health problems in later life.

When viewed in conjuction with our subject's innate sensitivity (7 & 9) and her desire to serve mankind within an organisation devoted to humanitarian causes (her Egoic Desire lesson), we note that her automatic response to any cry for help would be to take on an impossible workload and push her body beyond its limits in order to complete that task.

The role of the numerologist is to warn such individuals of the need to acknowledge the needs of their physical form, that it is not a sin to take a thirty minute rest from time to time to recharge their physical energy levels. Neither is it a sign of failure if they are unable to complete a task within a (self imposed) time limit.

Had the Physical Strength level of our subject been the greater there would have been no cause for alarm, for the lower level of her Vital Force would cause her to abandon a task long before her physical body had reached the point of exhaustion.

During a lecture tour of New Zealand some years ago I encountered a lady whose name serves to highlight a major problem for those having short or unusual names. I proffer the following as yet another example, well worth considering.

14 (5)	(5)	= 10 = 1 (**Spiritual Purpose**)
5 9	5	
NERRIS	**DERRY**	
5 99 1	4 99 7	
24 (6)	29 (11)	= 11 + 6 (**Egoic Desire**)
		= 11 + 7 (**Overall Self Exp'n.**)

Spiritual Purpose	=	1	Independence / Responsibility
Egoic Desire	= 11 + 6		Idealism expresed in loving & selfless committment to others
Overall Self Expression	= 11 + 7		Mediumistic ability utilised to aid the practical expression of idealistic endeavours.
Inspirational Capacity (7 & 9)	=	6	Highly intuitive with limited reasoning capacity.
Mental Power (1 & 8)	=	1	
Physical Strength (4 & 5)	=	4	Adequate strength levels but totally lacking in vitality.
Vital Force (2:3 & 6)	=	0	

Here we locate a hypersensitive person whose Spiritual Purpose lies in seeking independence and responsibility, leading others by the power of her example. However the Egoic Desire lesson makes this difficult to attain, for the extreme sensitivity which the 11 vibration brings about, coupled with the emotional responses stimulated by the number 6, may result in this person wishing to withdraw from the hustle and bustle of everyday life rather than playing a major role in shaping the lives of others. The Overall Self Expression lesson of 11 + 7 further accentuates her overly sensitive responses to the opinions of those around her, intensifying thereby her propensity for cloud dwelling.

This can also be observed in the ratio between the numbers relating to her Inspirational Capacity and Mental Power. The latter is virtually negligible whilst the former is quite high, increasing therefore her tendency to be highly strung.

However the purpose of this exercise is revealed by studying the ratio between the Physical Strength and Vital Force levels. Although her Physical Strength level is quite adequate our subject has no vitality whatsoever. This makes physical tasks difficult for she lacks the vigour with which to tackle them.

As the lady in question wished to know how she may create the necessary stimulus to enable her to live a full life I suggested that she might consider taking on an additional name, for provided that she utilised this in daily life, it could bring about the desired result. I might add that this is a solution I would only suggest when all else fails.

A problem then lay in finding the correct name, one which would not run counter to the rhythm of her life or intensify the difficulties she already faced. As she had a marked preference for a short name, one in keeping with her exisiting names, I finally suggested that she adopt a second forename and amend the spelling of her surname slightly. This would create a situation whereby her Physical Strength and Vital Force levels would become equal, enabling her to meet life's challenges with ease. Here an illustration of the amended life pattern will aid the student.

$$
\begin{array}{cccc}
14\,(5) & (9) & (1) & = 15 = 6 \\
5 \quad 9 & 9 & 1 &
\end{array}
$$

NERRIS-BRITT DARRY

$$
\begin{array}{ccc}
5 \quad 99 \ 1 \ 2 9 \ 22 \ 4 & 9 9 7 \\
24\,(6) \qquad 15\,(6) & 29\,(11) \qquad = 11 + 3
\end{array}
$$

$$
\overline{} \\
= 11 + 9
$$

Spiritual Purpose	= 6	Loving without condition
Egoic Desire	= 11 + 3	Expressing self and ideals in a practical manner
Overall Self Expression	= 11 + 9	Practical idealism expressed through service to mankind.
Inspirational Capacity (7 & 9)	= 8	Highly sensitive responses to everyday life. Intuitive.
Mental Power (1 & 8)	= 2	
Physical Strength (4 & 5)	= 3	Both aspects are now equal
Vital Force (2:3 & 6)	= 3	and balanced.

Such amendments are rarely achieved without cost as we note from this example, where a number of changes have been effected. Unfortunately, these have resulted in the ratio between the Inspirational Capacity and the Mental Power increasing in favour of the former, further intensifying our subject's level of sensitivity. The exercise has nonetheless brought about the balancing of the vital bodily energies and both the Physical Strength and Vital Force levels are now equal, enabling her to fullfil her daily tasks with a certain vigour.

These amendments to the name do of course change the Spiritual Purpose and Egoic Desire lessons. It now becomes necessary to counsel our subject on the necessity to remain earthed and to be practical in her approach to idealistic endeavours. It is also very important to stress that to be effective, these amendments to the name *must* be used each and every day. If our subject were not to insist on calling herself Nerris-Britt Darry then the exercise would serve no purpose.

Changing one's name is currently in vogue but it is not a practice I would personally advocate unless there are very powerful reasons for so doing. In many cases that I have encountered, it is the desire to avoid an unpleasant burden which causes many to undergo a change of name.

The subject of changing one's name automatically leads to the use of nicknames and the added responsibilities which women take upon themselves within marriage. These will be dealt with in the following chapter.

Workspace

Marriage Lessons and Nicknames

When two join together in holy matrimony it is not really an equal disposition of responsibility for it results in the female partner taking on an additional burden (which the sardonic may well consider to be the husband!) for she takes his name in addition to her own. Some may assume that this automatically frees her from the necessity to deal with the various lessons which lie within her original name, but alas, this is not so.

Rather, the wife embarks upon a period where she takes on greater responsibilites and is now expected to change the pattern of her life. The male partner makes no such change but fully expects his wife to adapt to his vibration. However in these days of female emancipation many women are breaking with tradition and insisting on retaining their own name, or that they they combine the surnames and both partners then accept a challenge.

Those ladies who select a number of husbands would appear to be possessed of a great desire to prove to all and sundry that they are equal to any challenge, despatching husbands at great speed. Some among them, in later life, begin to wonder which of their partners they will end up with in 'the great beyond' . . . but that is another subject!

Let us now consider another example in a bid to locate the lessons lying within the maiden name and then that taken on by marriage.

```
    (1)          15 (6)          (9)      = 16 = 7  Spiritual Purpose
    1           9   6           9
M A R Y   W I L S O N   S M I T H
4   9 7   5   3 1   5   1 4   2 8
    20 (2)       14 (5)          15 (6)   = 13 = 4  Egoic Desire
                                          ─────────
                                          11  Overall Self Exp.
```

The Higher Self of our subject is extremely sensitive, her Spiritual Purpose lesson amounting to 7 and she is possibly given to indulging in wild fantasies or vain illusions (the Danger Signal of 16). Unless these tendencies are brought under firm control they will result in a great deal of unhappiness when so many illusionary situations and friendships collapse around her.

The energy of the Egoic Desire lesson provides our subject with an extremely strong will (4) but as this arises from the Danger Signal 13 it also indicates a tendency to be rather careless in her approach to most matters in life. This person therefore needs to learn to remain focussed and to complete one task at a time. However, she expresses herself overall on the 11 vibration and this will intensify the dream-like quality of this lifetime, further accentuating her sensitivity.

If one day our subject encounters a 'knight on a white charger' by the name of Mr Green - and she believes all that he tells her without calling upon her intuitive powers (7) to check its veracity, the stage will be set for a traumatic marriage.

When seeking to locate the Marriage lesson, it matters not whether the numbers relating to the letters within it are placed above or below the name, for we are seeking its overall lesson. In this example our subject Mary Wilson Smith becomes Mary Wilson Green but it is only the new surname which concerns us here.

```
    GREEN
    7 9 5 5 5   = 31 = 4 = Marriage Lesson
```

Within this marriage our subject has chosen to demonstrate her practicality but may, at the outset, be faced with all manner of limitations particularly with regard to her personal liberty and freedom of expression. This in turn can lead to outright rebellion and deep resentment, particularly if her chosen partner is one who believes that a woman's place is in the home where she must be prepared to submit to the domination of the male. Surprisingly enough there are many who still subscribe to this outmoded tradition and who seek to enforce it. A good guideline for any bride-to-be is 'If he is possessive in courtship, he will be worse in marriage'.

The major obstacle to success in this union lies in the number of lessons which the number 4 will bring into being. The former Miss Smith will naturally rebel at the inordinate level of restriction placed upon her liberty and has to learn to reign-in her willpower as she seeks to steer the marriage toward a practical goal, within the rigid patterns laid down for her.

Despite this, our subject will experience a deal of difficulty in adapting to the lifestyle of her partner for she approached the whole concept in an idealistic manner, allowing illusion to colour her judgment.

Looking at the chart once more, note the two Danger Signals in her given names. The carelessness encouraged by the number 13 coupled with the illusionary element of the 16, together with the dream-like quality of the Over-Vibration of 11 provide a clear insight into her character. Miss Smith did not pay sufficient attention to detail (or her intuitive ability) before tying the knot, which may now be swiftly untied unless she comes to terms with the marriage lesson.

If she decides that this is all too difficult and cuts herself free from Mr Green, the lesson ceases with the divorce, *provided* that she also divests herself of his name. Failure to do so will ensure that the difficulties continue - which serves little purpose. If our subject then goes on to select another partner, a further lesson will commence with that marriage, hopefully with better results.

During the earlier part of this century it was common practice to give children a long string of names, more often than not to placate family members. As a result many were encumbered with names such as Gertrude Florence Hepzibah Patience Golightly. This practice resulted in great complexity for those so named who struggled to balance the often conflicting vibrations associated with the names they bore. To make matters worse the parents, regretting their well-intentioned act, proceed to call the child Daisy, a name she may then carry through life.

The usage of a nickname such as Daisy - or Dayse, even Dee makes the child's path through life even more arduous for it bestows yet another burden upon her and she begins to resemble a well-laden donkey who has to be goaded along the tortuous path of life. Let us take a look at this example to see what additional burdens she is being asked to carry.

DAISY
4 1 9 1 7   = 22 An exceptional challenge for she must strive to remain calm, cool and collected at all times. Difficult, given all those names.

DAYSE
4 1 7 1 5   = 9 A need to dedicate the self to serving others in a caring manner.

DEE
4 5 5   = (14) 5 Latent communication skills to be developed and thought patterns to be disciplined. The Danger Signal 14 will also encourage the tendency to be highly critical of others.

In the light of our discoveries it would appear to be more beneficial for our subject to revert to the use of Gertrude, despite its old-fashioned overtone, for it is a name which means 'Valkyrie', indicating that she incarnated to fight for her rights and demonstrate her courage. Daisy on the other hand means 'Miniature Sun' (which is possibly why her parents began to call her this).

Adoption of this name will result in her becoming the central source of light within her sphere of influence (her family by and large). Our subject may well prefer this course of action for it is far less challenging than that of the valkyrie. One further point well worth considering is that in dropping the name Daisy she eliminates the necessity to maintain perfect equilibrium within and without the self - a task most find too daunting.

Those among my readers who have been considering changing their name in any manner should carefully consider the information shared in this chapter. My recommendation would be to retain your original names and insist upon their use by those encountered in daily life, for no matter what, they indicate one's true pathway through life. Where it is a matter of marriage, discuss the matter with your husband-to-be and give consideration to using both names with a hyphen for your life together.

If on the other hand your knight on a white charger has become a knight errant, consider the value of his name. Does it benefit your overall lessons in life? Does it stimulate you to greater effort, or does it bring unnecessary restriction in its wake? If of benefit, retain it. If not, then discard it!

Work Space

Karmic Patterns

Have you ever puzzled over why your response to certain situations verges on the border of insanity? How, despite your best efforts, you tend to reflect your worst characteristics in a situation calling for a positive reaction? The answer lies hidden deep within your given names and relates to lessons which have been studiously avoided in former life experiences. These are termed Karmic Patterns and relate to the numbers which *do not appear* among those allocated to the letters within one's name. Let us return to the mythical Ms. McMillan in order to elucidate.

```
    5 1   9 5        9     1
    B E A T R I C E   M c M I L L A N
    2     2 9 3       4 3 4 3 3   5
```

Here you will note that I have ignored the sub-totals created during earlier exercises in order to arrive at the Spiritual Purpose and Egoic Desire lessons. Let us now study the numbers placed above and below the name to ascertain which numbers between one and nine are missing. Create a simple chart as illustrated below and note beside each one just how frequently they appear.

Number	Number	Number
1 - 2	4 - 2	7 - 0
2 - 2	5 - 3	8 - 0
3 - 4	6 - 0	9 - 3

This exercise reveals that the numbers 6: 7: and 8 do not appear at all indicating weaknesses which this person must strive to overcome during this incarnation (in addition to all other lessons shown in her chart!). On the following pages you may gain a measure of insight into the lessons which you yourself will encounter during your present life experience.

Returning to our example, it is evident that our subject will tend to keep her circle of friends small and will possibly meddle in their lives. She will also extricate herself very quickly from any undertaking or relationship once it becomes too onerous. Despite this trait she will be extremely possessive in friendships or relationships. These tendencies reflect the lack of experience with the number 6 in the past.

However, as our subject is hyper-sensitive possessed of a deep sense of inferiority (the lack of 7), she will tend to remain aloof from life in general which in turn will make for difficulty in forming meaningful relationships. Neither will she happily accept the many restrictions she will encounter in life. Indeed our subject will greet these with a measure of resentment whilst demonstrating a deal of impracticality with regard to monetary matters (the missing 8).

Fortunately this is a hypothetcial case and not one that any individual known to me would have the misfortune to undergo. Nonetheless those karmic lessons which apply to ourselves need to be viewed as valid experience and due attention given to them to ensure that they are overcome.

It may appear to the reader that life as illustrated here, is getting steadily more complicated page by page. However each of the lessons that await us in life form part of the necessary purification process that we volunteered to undergo and do not manifest as a quirk of fate. Knowledge of the pitfalls and potential weaknesses inherant within our natures will, I trust, stimulate the determination to overcome them.

Returning again to our example, it is possible to ascertain from the numbers which do appear, the manner in which our subject will respond to everyday situations.

```
   51    9 5        9   1

  BEATRICE    Mc MILLAN

   2     2 9 3     4 3 4  3 3    5
```

The number which appears most frequently within the name of our subject is 3, followed closely by the numbers 5 and 9, each of which appear three times.

As there is a strong emphasis on the number 3, our subject will long to express herself and play a part in social gatherings. Sadly her Karmic Patterns - particularly the number 7 will discourage participation in such events. In fact she may well become a shrinking violet, despite her inner desire. Being unable to mix as freely as she would wish, there may be a tendency to over indulge in alchohol or narcotics, leading eventually to deep cynicism or desperate unhappiness (the negative aspect of the 5).

The influence of the number 9 would stimulate a desire to render some form of service to mankind, yet her deep sense of inferiority (7), will prevent her from participation in those organisations which could so easily provide her with opportunities for self-expression.

Any refusal to play her part in life could result in the reflection of the destructive aspect of the numbers 1 and 4 which also appear in the chart. Where this occurs it will be reflected in her total dependence upon others coupled with a stubborn determination to involve herself only in those situations which have appeal. Behaviour of this nature may well result in this person returning at a later point in time to repeat these lessons.

Where any energy is missing from the name and the person concerned is faced with this as part of their date of birth, or as a marriage lesson, it will be difficult to master, for they have no previous experience of this particular energy.

Work Space

Name:

Number	Number	Number
1 - 2	4 - 2	7 - 0
2 - 2	5 - 3	8 - 0
3 - 4	6 - 0	9 - 3

Karmic Patterns:

Conclusion:

One

Making a stand or 'doing their own thing' totally independent of others will not come easily, if at all. Yet these are the very situations they will be expected to face at some point during their current life experience, having skilfully avoided both in the past.

'Independence' needs to become their rallying cry and with this will come the need to accept responsibility for their own thoughts and actions. Those who tend to be somewhat fainthearted with regard to decision making will also have to gather confidence in themselves and proceed to demonstrate to others just what they are capable of.

Two

Those who have avoided this lesson during former life experiences will be subject to excessive sensitivity, where a wrong word can trigger off an emotional outburst. This may be particularly marked in close relationships, within which they may undergo a deal of emotional trauma. If the current lifetime is to produce any worthwhile progression this over-sensitivity will need to be brought under firm control. Adapting to the will of those around and about may not be the easiest of tasks, yet this has to be accomplished - with a measure of diplomacy and tact.

On the mental level the mind may wander from the task in hand and minute details will be overlooked, (perhaps deliberately), for they will be considered to be unnecessary irritants by these individuals. Such weaknesses require a deal of attention and the determined development of the virtue of patience would prove to be a great asset.

Three

If these individuals could hide among the greenery at social functions they would gladly choose to do so for they feel inadequate when faced with strangers, lack social polish and are totally bereft of confidence in themselves or their abilities. As belief in ourselves is vital if we are to convince others, these individuals must pay a deal of attention to this aspect of their personality. In addition they need to understand how important personal appearances are and if they continue to dress as though they had hurriedly fitted themselves out at the local opportunity shop, they can expect to be ignored.

If they are to grow as individuals or achieve any meaningful success they have to learn to focus their attention upon one task at a time. Furthermore they should endeavour to perfect one particular quality or talent rather than channelling their energies into several avenues at much the same time.

Four

Here we locate the rebel without a cause who may expend a considerable amount of energy in avoiding a task or unwanted responsibility. These individuals are often strong- willed and stubborn, characteristics which reflect the negative aspect of Uranus. Practicality may not be their strong point yet it is something they should strive to develop, taking all limiting situations in their stride.

These individuals must 'get their act together' and develop their powers of concentration, particularly when faced with humdrum tasks. Self discipline and the acceptance of whatever situation they find themselves in will encourage others to view them in a more favourable light.

Five

An inability to let go of the past or any thing that they have outgrown, coupled with a great distaste for change, are traits which reflect the negative aspect of this vibration, as are glibness of tongue and deceit. Illusions of all kinds will dominate their thinking, particularly those of a sensual nature. These in turn may propel them toward frequent sexual encounters that may go hand in hand with over-indulgence in alchohol or narcotics.

Although these individals do have the potential to use their minds in a constructive manner, they will need to apply themselves to this task, applying the creative ideas which flood into their minds to the benefit of others.

Six

Among the lessons bypassed by these individuals in earlier incarnations is that appertaining to possessiveness. This trait will be particularly evident in their relationships, which may be of short duration because of this trait. As a result they may indulge in many transitory emotional encounters in their often desperate search for love. On the home front they may also be inclined to bemoan their lot in life having allowed others to burden them unduly.

Although they may have few real friends, they will continually interfere in their lives, ever on hand with a deal of unwanted advice, much of which they would do well to apply to their own lives. These individuals have little staying power and need to learn to follow through with whatever they commence and not abandon situations or undertakings once they become irksome.

Seven

An irrational fear of the unknown, over-sensitivity to everyday comment or situations, together with a tendency to remain aloof from those around and about them are all lessons side-stepped by these individuals in the past and which must now be overcome. A deep sense of inferiority (which in reality is an over-awareness of self) may also prevent growth as will a tendency to feel alone even in the midst of a crowd. Although they may indeed be different from those about them and possessed of unusual talents, until they learn to express these in a constructive manner, none will ever know.

Being impatient by nature, these individuals may be reluctant to apply themselves to spiritual disciplines such as meditation. They desire knowledge in abundance, but without recourse to arduous practices. Unless they overcome this weakness, the greater knowledge they seek will elude them.

Eight

No matter what measure of restraint or restriction these individuals encounter it is likely to be met with a murderous resentment, which in turn will serve to inflame an already difficult situation. Learning to come to terms with such obstacles will be a major lesson during this current lifetime. Initiations which they have deliberately avoided in the past now lie before them and these must be met (wherever possible) with a cheerful countenance, for the true victor is he or she who kneels in submission, accepting the inevitable.

Impracticality with regard to monetary matters will also be evident with money seeming to burn a hole in their pocket. As this is a vital energy they would do well to learn how to husband their monetary resources during this lifetime.

Nine

All of the negative traits which accompany the Martian energy will be evident here, being particularly demonstrated in their possessiveness toward loved ones or inanimate objects. Accompanying this will be a an explosive temperament, which must be brought under firm control if they are to experience a measure of happiness, for both traits serve to identify a deep sense of insecurity.

Many of those to whom this lesson applies will also be extremely selfish and if they are to avoid the self-created pits of despair they so often plunge into, they will need to look very carefully at the possibility of caring for others. Only through undertaking some form of selfless service, lovingly fulfilled without exacting a measure of return for their labours will they acquire a measure of personal satisfaction.

Setting Up A Chart

Having studied the many lessons associated with both the date of birth and names you bear, the next task lies in setting up a chart for another person. This must be concise in its direction not merely a series of snippets taken from different lessons, for that would merely confuse those you seek to help. Let us look once more at the example we have used throughout and note that the lessons are set out in order of their importance in the life of the individual concerned.

The Dynamics Of Self

$$20 = (2) \quad + \quad 10 = (1) \quad \text{———} \quad = \quad 3$$

5 1	9 5	9	1

BEATRICE   McMILLAN

2	29 3	434 33	5

$$16 = (7) \quad + \quad (22) \quad \text{———} \quad = 22 + 7$$

$$\text{Total:} = 22 = 1$$

Date of Birth: **12th JUNE 1963**

Reducing to: 3   6   (19)1   = 10 = 1

The Dynamics of Self

Governing Factor	=	3	= Self Expression
Destiny Factor	=	1	= Independent Action
Overall Self Expression	=	22 + 1	= Humanitarian leadership
Personality Factor	=	6	= Loving others without condition
Maturity Factor	=	(19) 1	= Responsibility and measure for measure
Spiritual Purpose	=	3	= Self Expression
Egoic Desire	=	22 + 7	= Practical visionary
Inspirational Capacity (7 & 9)	=	3	= Inclined to follow her intuition
Mental Power (1 & 8)	=	2	=
Physical Strength (4 & 5)	=	5	= Warning! Potential for over exertion.
Vital Force (2: 3 & 6)	=	6	=
Marriage Lesson			None
Adopted Name			None
Nickname			None
Karmic Lessons		6: 7: & 8	To be mastered

Interpretation.

The tone for this incarnation is set by the Governing Factor of 3 indicating a somewhat enjoyable lifetime, one filled with a great deal of social activity. Expansion and growth is the goal for this lifetime with the Ego finding expression in artistic or creative endeavours. A popular person, she should cultivate those influential people she encounters socially who will happily assist her with her expansionist plans. Being an independent thinker (the 1 of the Destiny Factor) she may well have to take the lead in creative enterprises.

The Overall Self - Expression lesson is best demonstrated

within a practical approach to situations of responsibility coupled with a balanced outlook upon life. From the age of twenty-eight onward the desire to be loved may over-ride all else and to this end our subject should learn to love others in an unconditional manner, avoiding wherever possible, the many emotional pitfalls which will manifest in her social life.

Once she reaches the age of fifty-six the Maturity Factor lesson will intensify the measure of responsibility this person will be expected to shoulder, together with much of the work-load in her environment. Any tendency to rest on her laurels could easily lead to the collapse of all that she has painstakingly built around her (the Danger Signal of 19).

The Higher Self of our subject also responds to the 3 vibration and this will intensify the desire to express the self creatively. However great care should be taken to ensure that such expression is of a practical nature at all times, for she will find illusionary pastimes highly attractive.

Being extremely sensitive and drawn to participate in humanitarian undertakings, this person would find a deal of personal satisfaction serving within a voluntary or charitable organisation wherein she could utilise her intuitive talent. As she will have a great deal of responsibility placed upon her shoulders within such organisations, she should take regular breaks from the stress of everyday life and learn to delegate authority.

Directly opposing the practical side of her nature is the irresponsible aspect which simply longs to enjoy life. This is encouraged by the Jupiterian influence which plays such a large part in her life via the number 3. This may lead to a deal of conflict within the self in respect of responsibility and practicality, especially as her Karmic lessons indicate a dislike of any form of restriction and impracticality with regard to monetary matters. She may also be rather possessive in her relationships and over-sensitive to criticism with a tendency to stand aloof from others.

Finally, as a Geminian our subject has to come to terms with the changeable energies of Mercury, learning to think before she speaks, and avoiding the tendency to flit from relationship to relationship or situation to situation. In her search for wisdom she will have to master the human aspect of her nature, learn to discern the false prophets (with regard to whom many a test lies in wait along her life-path). If this person is to attain her pre-determined goal for life, she will need to channel her energies into service-orientated undertakings.

In this manner the numerologist provides a clear and concise over-view of the life pattern ahead and for the Doubting Thomas's, contemplation of that which has already transpired to date will provide the individual concerned with sufficient proof of its accuracy.

Having pondered upon that which is set down within these pages, the student should now endeavour to put this knowledge into practice, enriching thereby the lives of those with whom they come into contact in daily life.

The Zodiac

The twin sciences of Numerology and Astrology should be viewed as equal parts of the whole when searching for the meaning of life, for together they serve to illustrate the pattern of the life ahead.

Astrological science has two aspects, Exoteric and Esoteric. The former illustrates the general characteristics of those who incarnate under the twelve major constellations, providing an insight into possible weaknesses and the many pitfalls that lie ahead, whilst the latter identifies the more challenging pathway back to the Godhead.

As we evolve through this Plane of Matter experiencing all that which the various constellations have to teach us, we slowly acquire awareness of our Higher Self and the purpose for repeated incarnations. This *exoteric* pathway through matter could be said to be relatively easy compared with that of *esoteric* progression in that the planetary energies do not at this point in our growth, hinder our progress.

Once the soul has learned all that it may from such experiences it is withdrawn to ponder upon the lessons it has learned and then returns to master the *esoteric* pathway, encountering en route all manner of difficulties and obstacles arising from its actions during earlier incarnations.

Throughout this book I have stressed the need for growth and development, indicating the potentials all may develop and in this final segment, I place a greater emphasis on the esoteric pathway. However I am not an astrologer and can at best provide a measure of insight for each constellation.

Aries

Ruling Planet: Mars
Element: Fire
Symbol: The Ram
21st March to 20th April

Here we encounter the spiritually awakened beings as they make their first appearance through the doorway of the Esoteric Zodiac. These are positive, daring individuals who are fully determined to succeed. However they can also be quite headstrong and tend to ignore pleas for caution, plunging repeatedly into challenging situations.

As the Esoteric Lesson for the sign of Aries lies within total mastery of thought, these individuals must swiftly come to an understanding of the limitless power of their mind and to use thought in a constructive manner at all times. Where this warning is ignored and thought is used in a destructive manner, its outcome will serve to firmly affix the unfortunate Ram to the Wheel of Life, ensuring constant return to matter until this particular lesson has been mastered.

In the Wisdom of The Ancients, thoughts were depicted as horses. Those which were uncontrollable reflected angry, bitter or resentful thought patterns whilst the calm, docile or harnessed horses represented mental energies which were being positively channelled.

According to Greek mythology, Diomedes, the son of Mars (the planetary ruler of the constellation of Aries) bred warhorses and when these escaped and began to breed with the wild horses of the plains, their offspring caused untold havoc. The Martian influence stimulates a fiery, warlike temperament and those born to experience this lesson should heed the symbolic message and gain firm control of their thought patterns.

Taurus

Ruling Planet: Venus
Element: Earth
Symbol: The Bull
21st April to 21st May

Those who appear under this constellation are as strong and dependable as the bull which identifies it, ever loyal to those with whom they form links of friendship. Taureans are much given to gazing over the fence at the grass on the other side, longing to taste its succulence yet, extremely wary of change, they remain with that which is familiar.

As Taurus is an earth sign, the majority of Taureans relate more readily to the world of matter than the realm of spirit. However Taureans need to come to terms with the fact that they do have a Higher Self and that one day the Bull (representing the Lower Self) must submit, accepting the measure of control the Higher Self seeks to exercise over their emotional expression. A deal of rebellion is to be expected before this may come about, coupled with a stubborn refusal to accept the necessity for change.

Yet the esoteric lesson these individuals have incarnated to master necessitates the raising of their level of consciousness beyond the mundane and the activation of their mystical Third Eye. Once activated, this will enable them to perceive for themselves the dimensions which lie beyond this Plane of Matter, bearing in mind the words of the Master ... "If thine eye be single then thy whole being shall be filled with light!".

Gemini

Ruling Planet: Mercury
Element::   Air
Symbol: The Twins
22nd May to 21st June

Five great tests await these freedom-loving individuals in
their search for wisdom, not the least of which is never to
accept defeat. The human aspect of their nature and its basic
desires will challenge them like some great serpent with
which they must be prepared to battle to the death.

With this conflict behind them, the Geminian must then be
on their guard for the false teacher who will appear to test
their ability to discern reality from illusion. He, she, or it
(for this may well be a book or false belief system) will
endeavour to restrict all independant thought or expression,
denying them the freedom so dear to the hearts of all born
under this constellation.

Having severed the ties which bound them to the false
prophet the Geminian will, despite their determination to
pursue their goal, attract toward them many individuals
who are lost or confused. Reluctant though they may be to put
the needs of others ahead of their search for wisdom, in so
doing their own goal will be brought tantalisingly close, only
to be set aside yet again when the greater problems of the
world loom large on the horizon. The overall lesson to be
absorbed by these individuals is that in placing the needs of
the many before the desires of the self, they will acquire the
wisdom they so fervently seek.

Cancer

Ruling Planet:: The Moon
Element: Water
Symbol: The Crab
22nd June to 23rd July

Secrecy and possessiveness are characteristics of this constellation and the pursuit of the unobtainable often results in emotional conflict and despair for the secretive Cancerian, who hides from view fearing rejection. Nonetheless they do emerge from time to time to grasp that which they desire. Whilst possession is nine-tenths of the law they will not benefit should they attempt to possess other individuals or to demand to be loved as a right.

Were the average Cancerian to apply a measure of stealth and tenacity to pursuing that which appertains to the Higher Self, untold misery on the personal level could be saved. Although deeply fearful, particularly of the unknown, these highly sensitive individuals should endeavour to develop the powerful intuitive faculty they possess and to then utilise this to guide the steps of the lost and the lonely.

This constellation has long been associated with the Christ Light (or Christos) and in ancient Egypt it was represented by the Scarab, which means 'Only Begotten'. If the Cancerian is prepared to accept the many cleansing situations or initiations that lie ahead as being a necessary impediment to further growth, and to love others without any expectation of return, then the Moon Child will take gigantic strides toward Self-realisation.

Leo

Ruling Planet::	**The Sun**
Element::	**Fire**
Symbol :	**The Lion**
24th July to 23rd August	

Pride stalks the lion as surely as any hunter. Having fashioned a powerful personality along with their 'coat of many colours' from the experiences of countless lifetimes, these individuals must now, of their own volition, undergo a form of self-crucifixion sacrificing the desires of the ego in a bid to follow the path of higher awareness. This will never be an easy decision for the proud Lion, indeed they may fight every inch of the way, roaring aloud their disapproval.

Long has the Leo personality ruled and held sway over other mortals and now comes the hour to acknowledge that a far greater force exists. In submitting, the Lion acknowledges its acceptance of the power of the Higher Self. The Leo may still roar from time to time to ensure that none forgets that the lion is king among lesser mortals, but all major opposition will have subsided.

Despite all the outer bravado, many Leo's are old softies or 'cowardy-custards' at heart who tend to hang back in the jungle of everyday life, never daring to raise their heads, let alone roar! But let there be no doubt, given the opportunity, coupled with a measure of self confidence, they too will seek to dominate others and the aforementioned lessons also apply to them.

Virgo

Ruling Planet: Mercury/Vulcan
Element: Earth
Symbol: The Virgin
24th August to 23rd September

Total equilibrium is the key which will unlock the Virgoan's greatest treasure - the mystical Third Eye - and repression of any aspect of the self will not provide any lasting solution. Such activity serves only to highlight a measure of imbalance within these individuals.

Gifted with a visionary ability the Virgoan may struggle long and hard to bring this to the point of fruition, defeated more often than not by their own puritanical points of view and critical faculty. In this they could be said to be their own worst enemy, for in turning that criticism on themselves they fashion an inferiority complex. As this indicates an over-awareness of self they should endeavour to cast aside their self-centred shackles and endeavour to 'see' with the *Eye of The Spirit*, utilising this to guide the steps of their less fortunate associates.

Virgoans are also gifted with lucid minds, creative natures, and possess a natural healing talent the use of which, coupled with their perceptive powers, can do much to improve the quality of life for humanity. In this task however they will need to overcome the influence of the co-ruler of this constellation, Vulcan. This is known as 'the planetary builder of form' and will stimulate over-awarness of physical problems, real or imaginary.

Libra

Ruling Planet :   Venus/Vesta
Element :   Air
Symbol :   The Scales
24th September to 23rd October

Those born under the Constellation of Libra incarnate in a bid to become balanced beings. As a result they tend to spend most of their lives weighing the pros and cons of every situation. This may result in marked changes of mood, positive and enthusiastic one moment and despairing the next.

This constellation, more than most within the Zodiac, brings great sadness to its natives for it is the clearing house, wherein they will be forced to meet the mistakes of the long-gone past head-on. The scales of Karma are heavily weighted against them for it is only through the philosophical acceptance of many traumatic experiences that they will develop the measure of equilibrium they seek.

Friendships will require careful scrutiny if the Libran is to avoid unnecessary hardships, but alas, it is their determination to emulate the Three Wise Monkeys which propels them into states of conflict. With the ability to see both sides of a situation they do tend to switch allegiance in the midst of controversial situations, and need to learn not to give their word until they have ascertained all relevant facts.

Librans are gifted peacemakers seeking to bring about balance in the lives of others and due to the influence of Venus, have a great appreciation of beauty, which is reflected within their tasteful home decor. Also possessed of strong mental powers they are avid for knowledge, but are particularly drawn toward the occult.

Scorpio

Ruling Planet:	**Pluto**
Element:	**Water**
Symbol:	**The Scorpion/Eagle**

24th October to 22nd November

The average Scorpio subject is much misunderstood. They battle their emotions - which are often at odds with the intellect - throughout life. As they tend to mask this conflict behind calm exteriors, few realise the extent of their problems. Fires may be burning below but the secretive Scorpio will never allow the world to know, for even if the ship is sinking they will give the indication that all is well.

These individuals have unusually retentive memories, particularly for past hurts, not one of which is ever forgotten. Although not aggressive by nature, those who provoke a Scorpion will learn to their cost that they can be quite relentless when seeking revenge.

Having elected to master their emotional nature during this lifetime, the evolved Scorpio must deal with the darker elements thereof which lurk beneath the surface. These range from cruelty to a desire for power and a love of comfort. There is also a strong interest in sexual matters and death.

Being a dual constellation, these naturally mediumistic individuals can, with determination, transmute their lower energies, transforming themselves in the process from the Scorpion whose sting lies within a sharp tongue, into the high-flying Golden Eagle. Their greatest difficulty lies in learning to accept the inevitable without rancour, which is the hallmark of the true initiate.

Sagittarius

Ruling Planet:	Jupiter
Element:	Fire
Symbol:	The Centaur
23rd November to 22nd December	

Many of those born to experience this constellation tend to sit on the fence for much of their lives, unable to make decisions and afraid to act. The same cannot be said of speech however, the majority being unable to curb their tongues. This in turn represents a major lesson for the Sagittarian who must come to terms with the power of the spoken word, learning to use few words rather than many. This equally applies to the power of thought, which in the average Sagittarian is an extremely potent force.

Ruled by the planet Jupiter they stand at the doorways of the Temples of Truth and Purification, for Jupiter encourages self-expression and expansion, particularly on the inner, mental level. The aspiration of the Sagittarian is usually high and with a measure of self-control, together with certain disciplines, they can do much to aid the evolution of mankind.

Having spent a number of incarnations within the ancient mystery schools and the cloisters of Christian orders, these individuals have the potential to reactivate part of the wisdom acquired therein. However they do need to learn to temper their enthusiasm when re-discovering a pearl of great price, for it reflects but a tiny fragment of the Ancient Wisdom. They should fire their arrows of aspiration toward the highest possible goal and, once achieved, become bearers of the light of truth.

Capricorn

Ruling Planet: Saturn
Element: Earth
Symbol: The Goat
23rd December to 20th January

A long and lonely road awaits the Goat as they endeavour to come to terms with the world of matter, for this being an Earth sign, these individuals will be acquisitive, surrounding themselves with earthly possessions and pursuing earthy pastimes. But in common with the goat which represents this constellation, they grow dissatisfied and seek ever higher pastures.

The unhappiness which dogs their path on the emotional level tends to turn these individuals into solitary beings, who find little humour in life. Yet it is important that they cultivate a sense of humour, for it is the hallmark of the true initiate which they must endeavour to become.

Deep within their subconscious memory lies a wealth of knowledge acquired during many lives devoted to the search for truth. Although it may prove a difficult task, the Capricornian should endeavour to place the needs of their Higher Self first, overcoming the pull of Earth and its many illusions.

The human aspect of their nature will present a great obstacle to such aspiration, for this constellation encourages the tendency to be unduly obstinate, mean and fearful. There is no easy pathway through life for the Capricornian, whether they follow their material or spiritual desires. Only through determined effort will they reach the proverbial mountain top and become the initiate.

Aquarius

Ruling Planet: Uranus/Saturn
Element: Air
Symbol: The Water Bearer
21st January to 19th February

The symbol of the Water Bearer clearly identifies the role of those born under this constellation - the showering of the waters of spiritual truth upon the fertile soil of awakened minds. Governed in part by by Uranus the Planet of the Will, these individuals will need to develop their mental powers if they are to achieve their goal. In ancient Greek mythology the mind was depicted as a midden filled with counter-productive thought patterns, which had to be cleansed with the Waters of Truth.

The majority of the human race will not welcome the altruistic attention of the Aquarian who should be prepared for a deal of rejection with regard to their New Age beliefs. Opposition of this nature reflects the restraining influence of the co-ruler of this sign, Saturn, who as the Great Initiator endeavours to test the mettle of the Aquarian.

This being a fixed Air sign, most Water Bearers tend to have a fixed outlook on life, although they are by nature cheerful individuals who mix easily with others. Uranus accentuates the power of the will and the Aquarian needs to learn not to abuse this potent energy.

Participation in groups formed of of like-minded individuals will enable the Aquarian to find expression for their innermost thoughts and aspiration, although personal needs or desires will have to be set aside in order that the group may attain its purpose.

Pisces

Ruling Planet: Jupiter/Neptune
Element: Water
Symbol: The Fish
20th February to 20th March

Due to the conflicting influence of the planets Jupiter and Neptune, a great many Pisceans fail to attain their intended goal in life. Jupiter encourages the pursuit of 'the good life' whilst the more intense vibrations of Neptune propel these individuals toward religious undertakings or contemplation of the inner reality.

The majority of Pisceans are highly sensitive and this being a Water sign, they can also be extremely emotional. The symbol of the two fish swimming in opposite directions clearly reflects their response to everyday life, being pulled in opposing directions simultaneously, for they are easily swayed by the opinons of stronger- willed individuals.

Pisces is the sign of The World Saviour, which is an enormous challenge for these sensitive individuals. They will constantly encounter those whose minds are blocked by narrow beliefs and the task of the Piscean is to attempt to bring the light of truth to closed minds.   This is an overwhelming responsibility under which the majority buckle.

In opposition, the negative aspect of their co-ruler Neptune will stimulate an emotional response to everyday events and subject them to all manner of illusion, particularly with regard to the self and its abilities. The Piscean must constantly stretch the self, reaching out to the Teachers on the higher sub-plane of the Mental Plane for the greater truths they require.

Second Sight

Throughout time those known to possess the gift of Second Sight have been held in awe - even feared - yet according to Edmund Harold this is a quality of the Soul and as such, ours by Divine Right. Each and every one of us has seven senses, the Sixth Sense being our Intuitive faculty and our Seventh Sense enables us to 'see' and communicate with the non-physical dimensions.

There are of course, many pitfalls along the way and these Edmund endeavours to highlight, whilst setting out a safe manner in which all who desire to expand their awareness beyond this three-dimensional Plane of Matter, may establish links with greater minds upon ever higher Planes of Consciousness, gaining thereby a deeper insight into their purpose in life.

The majority of higher communications are received in symbolic form and in order to be readily understood, these must first be translated. The would-be 'Seer' must therefore acquire a clear understanding of symbolism and Edmund Harold devotes a large part of this work to this all-important subject.

Other subjects covered in this fascinating book are Trance Channelling, Life After Death, Reincarnation, Earth-Bound Entities and Astral Travel.

Recommended retail price $19.95 (Australia)

Available from your local esoteric bookstore or direct from the publisher Grail Publications, P.O. Box 2316, Port Macquarie, NSW. 2444.

Vision Tomorrow

In an enthralling narrative Edmund Harold takes the reader through past, present and future scenarios, revealing through his clairvoyant faculty, images of cataclysmic earth changes to come.

Closely in line with predictions from sources as diverse as Astronomy and Geophysics, one must pay heed to the ever increasing body of informed opinion warning of difficult times ahead. Edmund Harold's prognosis is in essence an optimistic one. If we will heed the warnings in time, we have it in our power to influence the course of events.

Throughout the narrative Edmund also shares his experiences with The Brothers of the Light, non-physical beings who trained him throughout his childhood to become their channel in later life. Fascinating insights are given into a series of former life experiences commencing with the early stages of human evolution in Atlantis and onward to incarnations in Egypt, India and Tibet.

Originally published in 1981, a number of the situations forseen by Edmund Harold have now come to pass or are currently under way as the world and the human race faces ever more challenging situations,

An exciting book on many levels.

Recommended retail price $14.95 (Australia)

Available from your esoteric book stockist or direct from the publishers, Grail Publications, P. O. Box 2316, Port Macquarie,
N.S.W. 2444.

Crystal Healing

It is becoming more and more apparent that the humble quartz crystal has extraordinary properties. It can help heal the sick and improve the energies, concentration, decisiveness, empathetic qualities and state of balance of the healthy.

This 'modern discovery' is really a resurfacing of ancient knowledge, and, while the knowledge and use of quartz crystal power has had a continuous history ever since its ancient origins, it is now entering a renaissance. Much of what was lost is being slowly pieced together anew.

In Crystal Healing Edmund Harold addresses in particular the healing power of crystals, through discussion of the characteristics of the different types of crystals, how to select crystals and how to use them to achieve harmony of body and spirit.

Recommended retail price $19.95.

Available from your local book store.

Know Yourself, Heal Yourself

We all need a restoration of body and spirit at certain times in our lives, but how can we achieve it? Internationally known healer and lecturer Edmund Harold has brought together in this book information about a wide range of therapies that includes crystal healing, therapeutic touch (a kind of hands-on balancing technique), numerology, colour healing, music therapy, resonance therapy and astrology.

Know Yourself, Heal Yourself is invaluable for both lay person and healer; it will help those who wish to have a greater understanding of themselves (body, mind and spirit) and why they react to certain situations or conditions in a particular way; and it will direct those who wish to practice the art of healing.

As well as setting out clearly the philosophy behind each of the healing practices it describes, the book explores the practical aspects of working with people and 'energies'. Edmund Harold provides detailed descriptions of the various areas of the body involved in healing, such as the endocrine system, the chakras and the organ meridians. He gives numerous real-life examples from his thirty years experience in the field of natural healing therapy and many practical approaches to healing such as visualisation and guided imagery, meditation and crystal balancing.

Know Yourself, Heal Yourself is essential reading for those who wish to explore health and healing in its many aspects and for healers and aspiring practitioners.

Recommended retail price $19.95.

Available from your local bookstore.